Mometrix
TEST PREPARATION

Auctioneer Exam Secrets Study Guide

DEAR FUTURE EXAM SUCCESS STORY

First of all, **THANK YOU** for purchasing Mometrix study materials!

Second, congratulations! You are one of the few determined test-takers who are committed to doing whatever it takes to excel on your exam. **You have come to the right place.** We developed these study materials with one goal in mind: to deliver you the information you need in a format that's concise and easy to use.

In addition to optimizing your guide for the content of the test, we've outlined our recommended steps for breaking down the preparation process into small, attainable goals so you can make sure you stay on track.

We've also analyzed the entire test-taking process, identifying the most common pitfalls and showing how you can overcome them and be ready for any curveball the test throws you.

Standardized testing is one of the biggest obstacles on your road to success, which only increases the importance of doing well in the high-pressure, high-stakes environment of test day. Your results on this test could have a significant impact on your future, and this guide provides the information and practical advice to help you achieve your full potential on test day.

Your success is our success

We would love to hear from you! If you would like to share the story of your exam success or if you have any questions or comments in regard to our products, please contact us at **800-673-8175** or **support@mometrix.com**.

Thanks again for your business and we wish you continued success!

Sincerely,
The Mometrix Test Preparation Team

Written and edited by the Mometrix Exam Secrets Test Prep Team
Printed in the United States of America

TABLE OF CONTENTS

Introduction

Thank you for purchasing this resource! You have made the choice to prepare yourself for a test that could have a huge impact on your future, and this guide is designed to help you be fully ready for test day. Obviously, it's important to have a solid understanding of the test material, but you also need to be prepared for the unique environment and stressors of the test, so that you can perform to the best of your abilities.

For this purpose, the first section that appears in this guide is the **Secret Keys**. We've devoted countless hours to meticulously researching what works and what doesn't, and we've boiled down our findings to the five most impactful steps you can take to improve your performance on the test. We start at the beginning with study planning and move through the preparation process, all the way to the testing strategies that will help you get the most out of what you know when you're finally sitting in front of the test.

We recommend that you start preparing for your test as far in advance as possible. However, if you've bought this guide as a last-minute study resource and only have a few days before your test, we recommend that you skip over the first two Secret Keys since they address a long-term study plan.

If you struggle with **test anxiety**, we strongly encourage you to check out our recommendations for how you can overcome it. Test anxiety is a formidable foe, but it can be beaten, and we want to make sure you have the tools you need to defeat it.

Secret Key 1: Plan Big, Study Small

There's a lot riding on your performance. If you want to ace this test, you're going to need to keep your skills sharp and the material fresh in your mind. You need a plan that lets you review everything you need to know while still fitting in your schedule. We'll break this strategy down into three categories.

Information Organization

Start with the information you already have: the official test outline. From this, you can make a complete list of all the concepts you need to cover before the test. Organize these concepts into groups that can be studied together, and create a list of any related vocabulary you need to learn so you can brush up on any difficult terms. You'll want to keep this vocabulary list handy once you actually start studying since you may need to add to it along the way.

Time Management

Once you have your set of study concepts, decide how to spread them out over the time you have left before the test. Break your study plan into small, clear goals so you have a manageable task for each day and know exactly what you're doing. Then just focus on one small step at a time. When you manage your time this way, you don't need to spend hours at a time studying. Studying a small block of content for a short period each day helps you retain information better and avoid stressing over how much you have left to do. You can relax knowing that you have a plan to cover everything in time. In order for this strategy to be effective though, you have to start studying early and stick to your schedule. Avoid the exhaustion and futility that comes from last-minute cramming!

Study Environment

The environment you study in has a big impact on your learning. Studying in a coffee shop, while probably more enjoyable, is not likely to be as fruitful as studying in a quiet room. It's important to keep distractions to a minimum. You're only planning to study for a short block of time, so make the most of it. Don't pause to check your phone or get up to find a snack. It's also important to **avoid multitasking**. Research has consistently shown that multitasking will make your studying dramatically less effective. Your study area should also be comfortable and well-lit so you don't have the distraction of straining your eyes or sitting on an uncomfortable chair.

The time of day you study is also important. You want to be rested and alert. Don't wait until just before bedtime. Study when you'll be most likely to comprehend and remember. Even better, if you know what time of day your test will be, set that time aside for study. That way your brain will be used to working on that subject at that specific time and you'll have a better chance of recalling information.

Finally, it can be helpful to team up with others who are studying for the same test. Your actual studying should be done in as isolated an environment as possible, but the work of organizing the information and setting up the study plan can be divided up. In between study sessions, you can discuss with your teammates the concepts that you're all studying and quiz each other on the details. Just be sure that your teammates are as serious about the test as you are. If you find that your study time is being replaced with social time, you might need to find a new team.

Secret Key 2: Make Your Studying Count

You're devoting a lot of time and effort to preparing for this test, so you want to be absolutely certain it will pay off. This means doing more than just reading the content and hoping you can remember it on test day. It's important to make every minute of study count. There are two main areas you can focus on to make your studying count.

Retention

It doesn't matter how much time you study if you can't remember the material. You need to make sure you are retaining the concepts. To check your retention of the information you're learning, try recalling it at later times with minimal prompting. Try carrying around flashcards and glance at one or two from time to time or ask a friend who's also studying for the test to quiz you.

To enhance your retention, look for ways to put the information into practice so that you can apply it rather than simply recalling it. If you're using the information in practical ways, it will be much easier to remember. Similarly, it helps to solidify a concept in your mind if you're not only reading it to yourself but also explaining it to someone else. Ask a friend to let you teach them about a concept you're a little shaky on (or speak aloud to an imaginary audience if necessary). As you try to summarize, define, give examples, and answer your friend's questions, you'll understand the concepts better and they will stay with you longer. Finally, step back for a big picture view and ask yourself how each piece of information fits with the whole subject. When you link the different concepts together and see them working together as a whole, it's easier to remember the individual components.

Finally, practice showing your work on any multi-step problems, even if you're just studying. Writing out each step you take to solve a problem will help solidify the process in your mind, and you'll be more likely to remember it during the test.

Modality

Modality simply refers to the means or method by which you study. Choosing a study modality that fits your own individual learning style is crucial. No two people learn best in exactly the same way, so it's important to know your strengths and use them to your advantage.

For example, if you learn best by visualization, focus on visualizing a concept in your mind and draw an image or a diagram. Try color-coding your notes, illustrating them, or creating symbols that will trigger your mind to recall a learned concept. If you learn best by hearing or discussing information, find a study partner who learns the same way or read aloud to yourself. Think about how to put the information in your own words. Imagine that you are giving a lecture on the topic and record yourself so you can listen to it later.

For any learning style, flashcards can be helpful. Organize the information so you can take advantage of spare moments to review. Underline key words or phrases. Use different colors for different categories. Mnemonic devices (such as creating a short list in which every item starts with the same letter) can also help with retention. Find what works best for you and use it to store the information in your mind most effectively and easily.

Secret Key 3: Practice the Right Way

Your success on test day depends not only on how many hours you put into preparing, but also on whether you prepared the right way. It's good to check along the way to see if your studying is paying off. One of the most effective ways to do this is by taking practice tests to evaluate your progress. Practice tests are useful because they show exactly where you need to improve. Every time you take a practice test, pay special attention to these three groups of questions:

- The questions you got wrong
- The questions you had to guess on, even if you guessed right
- The questions you found difficult or slow to work through

This will show you exactly what your weak areas are, and where you need to devote more study time. Ask yourself why each of these questions gave you trouble. Was it because you didn't understand the material? Was it because you didn't remember the vocabulary? Do you need more repetitions on this type of question to build speed and confidence? Dig into those questions and figure out how you can strengthen your weak areas as you go back to review the material.

Additionally, many practice tests have a section explaining the answer choices. It can be tempting to read the explanation and think that you now have a good understanding of the concept. However, an explanation likely only covers part of the question's broader context. Even if the explanation makes perfect sense, **go back and investigate** every concept related to the question until you're positive you have a thorough understanding.

As you go along, keep in mind that the practice test is just that: practice. Memorizing these questions and answers will not be very helpful on the actual test because it is unlikely to have any of the same exact questions. If you only know the right answers to the sample questions, you won't be prepared for the real thing. **Study the concepts** until you understand them fully, and then you'll be able to answer any question that shows up on the test.

It's important to wait on the practice tests until you're ready. If you take a test on your first day of study, you may be overwhelmed by the amount of material covered and how much you need to learn. Work up to it gradually.

On test day, you'll need to be prepared for answering questions, managing your time, and using the test-taking strategies you've learned. It's a lot to balance, like a mental marathon that will have a big impact on your future. Like training for a marathon, you'll need to start slowly and work your way up. When test day arrives, you'll be ready.

Start with the strategies you've read in the first two Secret Keys—plan your course and study in the way that works best for you. If you have time, consider using multiple study resources to get different approaches to the same concepts. It can be helpful to see difficult concepts from more than one angle. Then find a good source for practice tests. Many times, the test website will suggest potential study resources or provide sample tests.

Practice Test Strategy

If you're able to find at least three practice tests, we recommend this strategy:

Untimed and Open-Book Practice

Take the first test with no time constraints and with your notes and study guide handy. Take your time and focus on applying the strategies you've learned.

Timed and Open-Book Practice

Take the second practice test open-book as well, but set a timer and practice pacing yourself to finish in time.

Timed and Closed-Book Practice

Take any other practice tests as if it were test day. Set a timer and put away your study materials. Sit at a table or desk in a quiet room, imagine yourself at the testing center, and answer questions as quickly and accurately as possible.

Keep repeating timed and closed-book tests on a regular basis until you run out of practice tests or it's time for the actual test. Your mind will be ready for the schedule and stress of test day, and you'll be able to focus on recalling the material you've learned.

Secret Key 4: Pace Yourself

Once you're fully prepared for the material on the test, your biggest challenge on test day will be managing your time. Just knowing that the clock is ticking can make you panic even if you have plenty of time left. Work on pacing yourself so you can build confidence against the time constraints of the exam. Pacing is a difficult skill to master, especially in a high-pressure environment, so **practice is vital**.

Set time expectations for your pace based on how much time is available. For example, if a section has 60 questions and the time limit is 30 minutes, you know you have to average 30 seconds or less per question in order to answer them all. Although 30 seconds is the hard limit, set 25 seconds per question as your goal, so you reserve extra time to spend on harder questions. When you budget extra time for the harder questions, you no longer have any reason to stress when those questions take longer to answer.

Don't let this time expectation distract you from working through the test at a calm, steady pace, but keep it in mind so you don't spend too much time on any one question. Recognize that taking extra time on one question you don't understand may keep you from answering two that you do understand later in the test. If your time limit for a question is up and you're still not sure of the answer, mark it and move on, and come back to it later if the time and the test format allow. If the testing format doesn't allow you to return to earlier questions, just make an educated guess; then put it out of your mind and move on.

On the easier questions, be careful not to rush. It may seem wise to hurry through them so you have more time for the challenging ones, but it's not worth missing one if you know the concept and just didn't take the time to read the question fully. Work efficiently but make sure you understand the question and have looked at all of the answer choices, since more than one may seem right at first.

Even if you're paying attention to the time, you may find yourself a little behind at some point. You should speed up to get back on track, but do so wisely. Don't panic; just take a few seconds less on each question until you're caught up. Don't guess without thinking, but do look through the answer choices and eliminate any you know are wrong. If you can get down to two choices, it is often worthwhile to guess from those. Once you've chosen an answer, move on and don't dwell on any that you skipped or had to hurry through. If a question was taking too long, chances are it was one of the harder ones, so you weren't as likely to get it right anyway.

On the other hand, if you find yourself getting ahead of schedule, it may be beneficial to slow down a little. The more quickly you work, the more likely you are to make a careless mistake that will affect your score. You've budgeted time for each question, so don't be afraid to spend that time. Practice an efficient but careful pace to get the most out of the time you have.

Secret Key 5: Have a Plan for Guessing

When you're taking the test, you may find yourself stuck on a question. Some of the answer choices seem better than others, but you don't see the one answer choice that is obviously correct. What do you do?

The scenario described above is very common, yet most test takers have not effectively prepared for it. Developing and practicing a plan for guessing may be one of the single most effective uses of your time as you get ready for the exam.

In developing your plan for guessing, there are three questions to address:

- When should you start the guessing process?
- How should you narrow down the choices?
- Which answer should you choose?

When to Start the Guessing Process

Unless your plan for guessing is to select C every time (which, despite its merits, is not what we recommend), you need to leave yourself enough time to apply your answer elimination strategies. Since you have a limited amount of time for each question, that means that if you're going to give yourself the best shot at guessing correctly, you have to decide quickly whether or not you will guess.

Of course, the best-case scenario is that you don't have to guess at all, so first, see if you can answer the question based on your knowledge of the subject and basic reasoning skills. Focus on the key words in the question and try to jog your memory of related topics. Give yourself a chance to bring the knowledge to mind, but once you realize that you don't have (or you can't access) the knowledge you need to answer the question, it's time to start the guessing process.

It's almost always better to start the guessing process too early than too late. It only takes a few seconds to remember something and answer the question from knowledge. Carefully eliminating wrong answer choices takes longer. Plus, going through the process of eliminating answer choices can actually help jog your memory.

Summary: Start the guessing process as soon as you decide that you can't answer the question based on your knowledge.

How to Narrow Down the Choices

The next chapter in this book (**Test-Taking Strategies**) includes a wide range of strategies for how to approach questions and how to look for answer choices to eliminate. You will definitely want to read those carefully, practice them, and figure out which ones work best for you. Here though, we're going to address a mindset rather than a particular strategy.

Your odds of guessing an answer correctly depend on how many options you are choosing from.

Number of options left	5	4	3	2	1
Odds of guessing correctly	20%	25%	33%	50%	100%

You can see from this chart just how valuable it is to be able to eliminate incorrect answers and make an educated guess, but there are two things that many test takers do that cause them to miss out on the benefits of guessing:

- Accidentally eliminating the correct answer
- Selecting an answer based on an impression

We'll look at the first one here, and the second one in the next section.

To avoid accidentally eliminating the correct answer, we recommend a thought exercise called **the $5 challenge**. In this challenge, you only eliminate an answer choice from contention if you are willing to bet $5 on it being wrong. Why $5? Five dollars is a small but not insignificant amount of money. It's an amount you could afford to lose but wouldn't want to throw away. And while losing $5 once might not hurt too much, doing it twenty times will set you back $100. In the same way, each small decision you make—eliminating a choice here, guessing on a question there—won't by itself impact your score very much, but when you put them all together, they can make a big difference. By holding each answer choice elimination decision to a higher standard, you can reduce the risk of accidentally eliminating the correct answer.

The $5 challenge can also be applied in a positive sense: If you are willing to bet $5 that an answer choice *is* correct, go ahead and mark it as correct.

Summary: Only eliminate an answer choice if you are willing to bet $5 that it is wrong.

Which Answer to Choose

You're taking the test. You've run into a hard question and decided you'll have to guess. You've eliminated all the answer choices you're willing to bet $5 on. Now you have to pick an answer. Why do we even need to talk about this? Why can't you just pick whichever one you feel like when the time comes?

The answer to these questions is that if you don't come into the test with a plan, you'll rely on your impression to select an answer choice, and if you do that, you risk falling into a trap. The test writers know that everyone who takes their test will be guessing on some of the questions, so they intentionally write wrong answer choices to seem plausible. You still have to pick an answer though, and if the wrong answer choices are designed to look right, how can you ever be sure that you're not falling for their trap? The best solution we've found to this dilemma is to take the decision out of your hands entirely. Here is the process we recommend:

Once you've eliminated any choices that you are confident (willing to bet $5) are wrong, select the first remaining choice as your answer.

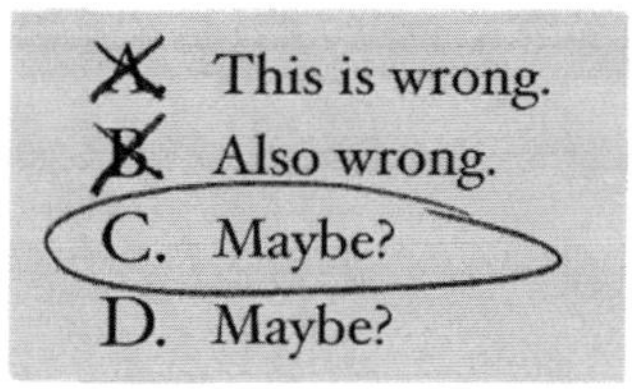

Whether you choose to select the first remaining choice, the second, or the last, the important thing is that you use some preselected standard. Using this approach guarantees that you will not be enticed into selecting an answer choice that looks right, because you are not basing your decision on how the answer choices look.

This is not meant to make you question your knowledge. Instead, it is to help you recognize the difference between your knowledge and your impressions. There's a huge difference between thinking an answer is right because of what you know, and thinking an answer is right because it looks or sounds like it should be right.

Summary: To ensure that your selection is appropriately random, make a predetermined selection from among all answer choices you have not eliminated.

Test-Taking Strategies

This section contains a list of test-taking strategies that you may find helpful as you work through the test. By taking what you know and applying logical thought, you can maximize your chances of answering any question correctly!

It is very important to realize that every question is different and every person is different: no single strategy will work on every question, and no single strategy will work for every person. That's why we've included all of them here, so you can try them out and determine which ones work best for different types of questions and which ones work best for you.

Question Strategies

✅ Read Carefully

Read the question and the answer choices carefully. Don't miss the question because you misread the terms. You have plenty of time to read each question thoroughly and make sure you understand what is being asked. Yet a happy medium must be attained, so don't waste too much time. You must read carefully and efficiently.

✅ Contextual Clues

Look for contextual clues. If the question includes a word you are not familiar with, look at the immediate context for some indication of what the word might mean. Contextual clues can often give you all the information you need to decipher the meaning of an unfamiliar word. Even if you can't determine the meaning, you may be able to narrow down the possibilities enough to make a solid guess at the answer to the question.

✅ Prefixes

If you're having trouble with a word in the question or answer choices, try dissecting it. Take advantage of every clue that the word might include. Prefixes can be a huge help. Usually, they allow you to determine a basic meaning. *Pre-* means before, *post-* means after, *pro-* is positive, *de-* is negative. From prefixes, you can get an idea of the general meaning of the word and try to put it into context.

✅ Hedge Words

Watch out for critical hedge words, such as *likely, may, can, often, almost, mostly, usually, generally, rarely,* and *sometimes.* Question writers insert these hedge phrases to cover every possibility. Often an answer choice will be wrong simply because it leaves no room for exception. Be on guard for answer choices that have definitive words such as *exactly* and *always.*

☑ Switchback Words

Stay alert for *switchbacks*. These are the words and phrases frequently used to alert you to shifts in thought. The most common switchback words are *but*, *although*, and *however*. Others include *nevertheless, on the other hand, even though, while, in spite of, despite*, and *regardless of*. Switchback words are important to catch because they can change the direction of the question or an answer choice.

☑ Face Value

When in doubt, use common sense. Accept the situation in the problem at face value. Don't read too much into it. These problems will not require you to make wild assumptions. If you have to go beyond creativity and warp time or space in order to have an answer choice fit the question, then you should move on and consider the other answer choices. These are normal problems rooted in reality. The applicable relationship or explanation may not be readily apparent, but it is there for you to figure out. Use your common sense to interpret anything that isn't clear.

Answer Choice Strategies

☑ Answer Selection

The most thorough way to pick an answer choice is to identify and eliminate wrong answers until only one is left, then confirm it is the correct answer. Sometimes an answer choice may immediately seem right, but be careful. The test writers will usually put more than one reasonable answer choice on each question, so take a second to read all of them and make sure that the other choices are not equally obvious. As long as you have time left, it is better to read every answer choice than to pick the first one that looks right without checking the others.

☑ Answer Choice Families

An answer choice family consists of two (in rare cases, three) answer choices that are very similar in construction and cannot all be true at the same time. If you see two answer choices that are direct opposites or parallels, one of them is usually the correct answer. For instance, if one answer choice says that quantity *x* increases and another either says that quantity *x* decreases (opposite) or says that quantity *y* increases (parallel), then those answer choices would fall into the same family. An answer choice that doesn't match the construction of the answer choice family is more likely to be incorrect. Most questions will not have answer choice families, but when they do appear, you should be prepared to recognize them.

☑ Eliminate Answers

Eliminate answer choices as soon as you realize they are wrong, but make sure you consider all possibilities. If you are eliminating answer choices and realize that the last one you are left with is also wrong, don't panic. Start over and consider each choice again. There may be something you missed the first time that you will realize on the second pass.

⊘ Avoid Fact Traps

Don't be distracted by an answer choice that is factually true but doesn't answer the question. You are looking for the choice that answers the question. Stay focused on what the question is asking for so you don't accidentally pick an answer that is true but incorrect. Always go back to the question and make sure the answer choice you've selected actually answers the question and is not merely a true statement.

⊘ Extreme Statements

In general, you should avoid answers that put forth extreme actions as standard practice or proclaim controversial ideas as established fact. An answer choice that states the "process should be used in certain situations, if..." is much more likely to be correct than one that states the "process should be discontinued completely." The first is a calm rational statement and doesn't even make a definitive, uncompromising stance, using a hedge word *if* to provide wiggle room, whereas the second choice is far more extreme.

⊘ Benchmark

As you read through the answer choices and you come across one that seems to answer the question well, mentally select that answer choice. This is not your final answer, but it's the one that will help you evaluate the other answer choices. The one that you selected is your benchmark or standard for judging each of the other answer choices. Every other answer choice must be compared to your benchmark. That choice is correct until proven otherwise by another answer choice beating it. If you find a better answer, then that one becomes your new benchmark. Once you've decided that no other choice answers the question as well as your benchmark, you have your final answer.

⊘ Predict the Answer

Before you even start looking at the answer choices, it is often best to try to predict the answer. When you come up with the answer on your own, it is easier to avoid distractions and traps because you will know exactly what to look for. The right answer choice is unlikely to be word-for-word what you came up with, but it should be a close match. Even if you are confident that you have the right answer, you should still take the time to read each option before moving on.

General Strategies

⊘ Tough Questions

If you are stumped on a problem or it appears too hard or too difficult, don't waste time. Move on! Remember though, if you can quickly check for obviously incorrect answer choices, your chances of guessing correctly are greatly improved. Before you completely give up, at least try to knock out a couple of possible answers. Eliminate what you can and then guess at the remaining answer choices before moving on.

☑ CHECK YOUR WORK

Since you will probably not know every term listed and the answer to every question, it is important that you get credit for the ones that you do know. Don't miss any questions through careless mistakes. If at all possible, try to take a second to look back over your answer selection and make sure you've selected the correct answer choice and haven't made a costly careless mistake (such as marking an answer choice that you didn't mean to mark). This quick double check should more than pay for itself in caught mistakes for the time it costs.

☑ PACE YOURSELF

It's easy to be overwhelmed when you're looking at a page full of questions; your mind is confused and full of random thoughts, and the clock is ticking down faster than you would like. Calm down and maintain the pace that you have set for yourself. Especially as you get down to the last few minutes of the test, don't let the small numbers on the clock make you panic. As long as you are on track by monitoring your pace, you are guaranteed to have time for each question.

☑ DON'T RUSH

It is very easy to make errors when you are in a hurry. Maintaining a fast pace in answering questions is pointless if it makes you miss questions that you would have gotten right otherwise. Test writers like to include distracting information and wrong answers that seem right. Taking a little extra time to avoid careless mistakes can make all the difference in your test score. Find a pace that allows you to be confident in the answers that you select.

☑ KEEP MOVING

Panicking will not help you pass the test, so do your best to stay calm and keep moving. Taking deep breaths and going through the answer elimination steps you practiced can help to break through a stress barrier and keep your pace.

Final Notes

The combination of a solid foundation of content knowledge and the confidence that comes from practicing your plan for applying that knowledge is the key to maximizing your performance on test day. As your foundation of content knowledge is built up and strengthened, you'll find that the strategies included in this chapter become more and more effective in helping you quickly sift through the distractions and traps of the test to isolate the correct answer.

Now that you're preparing to move forward into the test content chapters of this book, be sure to keep your goal in mind. As you read, think about how you will be able to apply this information on the test. If you've already seen sample questions for the test and you have an idea of the question format and style, try to come up with questions of your own that you can answer based on what you're reading. This will give you valuable practice applying your knowledge in the same ways you can expect to on test day.

Good luck and good studying!

Auctioneer Exam

An **auction** is a method of selling real property, personal property or other goods in a public arena. Buyers bid against each other in open competition for items or lots. The lot is sold to the bidder who offers the highest price.

The **auctioneer** is the person who plans, advertises and executes the sale, calls the bids, announces the buyer and closes the sale. The auctioneer is licensed by the state and in most states is required to pass a written examination. The auctioneer must comply with the rules and regulations mandated by the state in which the license is granted and the auction is being held. Some states require periodic renewal of the auctioneer's license.

The **seller**, also called the client, is the person who authorizes the sale of the property. The **buyer**, also called the customer or bidder, is a person who is qualified to buy the item offered for sale.

There are many different types of auctions. An **absolute** auction, also called an auction without reserve, means the item is sold to the qualified bidder who offers the highest price. There are no limits or conditions on the amount of the bid. The seller or agent may not bid on the item.

A **minimum bid** auction means the starting bid has been set at a certain number. The minimum bid is published in the brochure and any advertisements prior to the auction. The auctioneer announces the minimum required bid before the actual bidding begins.

A **reserve** auction, also called an auction with reserve or an auction subject to confirmation means the seller or agent has the right to set a minimum bid, to accept or decline any bids offered and to withdraw the item any time before the auctioneer declares the sale complete. The minimum price may or may not have been published.

A **catalogue** auction is conducted in a place separate from where the sale items are stored. Interested buyers need to inspect the goods prior to sale day. The auctioneer should include the day(s), date(s), time(s) and exact location of where the sale items are available for inspection in all advertising media.

An **on-site** auction is conducted at the location where the goods are stored. One reason for this type of auction is when a business is in liquidation and it may not be easy or practical to move the inventory, furniture, equipment, etc. to another location.

At a **Dutch** auction, the seller offers multiples of the same item for sale. Every winning bidder pays the lowest successful bid. At a **Yankee** auction, the seller offers multiples of the same item for sale. Each winning bidder pays his or her successful bid.

Auction Terms

As Is: When an item is sold without any guarantee as to condition, usefulness, or contents (in some cases), it is sold "as is." It is the buyer's responsibility to determine the condition of the item. The terms "as is", "where is" and "in its present condition" are also used and mean the same thing.

Auction Listing Agreement: The Auction Listing Agreement is a contract between the seller and the auctioneer. This legal document authorizes the auctioneer to sell the property for the seller and spells out the specific terms of the agreement. The rights and responsibilities of both parties and the distribution of the proceeds of the sale are clearly defined.

Agent: Sellers and buyers can appoint an agent as their representative. The agent handles the details of sale. In some states, the same agent cannot represent the seller and buyer of the same property without a signed disclosure statement.

Bids

When a potential buyer indicates a specific price he or she willing pay for an item, this is called a bid. An absentee bid is a specific procedure that allows a potential buyer to participate in the bidding process without actually being present at the auction. The auctioneer sets absentee bid guidelines before the auction begins. Some states require the guidelines be published prior to the start of the auction. The buyer's premium is either a percentage of the winning bid or a flat fee that is added to the final price the buyer is required to pay for the item.

The reserve bid is the minimum price a seller is willing to accept for the item. It is also called the reserve price.

Auction Advantages

Placing a classified ad in a local newspaper or a "for sale by owner" (FSBO) sign in the front yard or in the back window of the vehicle may attract a few lookers but no serious takers. Finding the right buyer could take weeks or months. In addition, the seller may be forced to accept less than the item is worth. Auctions offer a unique way to determine the true market value for the item and usually generate interest and excitement. Effective advertising in various media geared toward a target audience brings together motivated people interested in buying what other people have to sell. The enthusiasm of the auctioneer's chant combined with creative pre-auction marketing plus the competitive bidding at the auction itself often generates a higher price than expected.

There are various reasons why a seller offers his property for sale at an auction. The ones listed below are merely a sample.

- To pay off debts due to liquidation, receivership or bankruptcy.
- Disposal of an estate.
- To make a profit.
- Make room for new inventory.

- Dispose of extra or surplus items that cannot be returned to the manufacturer.
- Items (furniture, equipment) part of a lease and the leasing company doesn't want them back.
- Items that won't sell because of low demand or over supply.
- Contraband confiscated by a federal, state or local government agency.
- Stolen items whose original owners cannot be found.

Anything can be offered for sale at auctions by owners for many reasons. Local newspapers and various web sites list what is being offered, by whom, when and where. Here is a partial list of items that can be offered at auction:

- Antique furniture, jewelry, china and glassware.
- Paintings and sculptures.
- Various collectibles such as stamps, coins, books, magazines, dolls, etc.
- Real property: single family homes, apartment buildings, commercial buildings, undeveloped land.
- Large and small appliances, electronic equipment, furniture, carpet.
- Food, beer, wine, liquor.
- Office furniture and equipment.
- Home and business computer and phone systems.
- Classic and vintage cars, trucks, farm and industrial equipment and machinery.
- New and used cars, vans, heavy and light trucks.
- Livestock: cattle, horses, goats, pigs, poultry, etc.
- New and used farm equipment.
- Items confiscated by federal, state and local governments.

Values

One factor in determining the worth of the property is the current market for the item being offered. For example, the value of real estate (i.e. undeveloped land, private homes, commercial property, etc.) is based on the specific location and the average sales price of similar property in that locality. Specialized commodities like industry-specific machinery, office furniture, jewelry and collectibles appeal to a smaller group but the potential buyers are not confined to one geographic area.

The condition of the property, its age, manufacturer (if applicable), repairs that might be needed before it can be used, available records such as maintenance logs and receipts for improvements and repairs are all factored into determining the value of the property.

Ways to check the value of similar items include but are not limited to: contacting retail stores and consignment and re-sale shops, reading newspaper classified sections and searching reliable Internet sites.

Appraisals

To appraise means to inspect, evaluate and place a monetary value on an item. An appraisal is a judgment or opinion of what the item is worth. The person appraising the item should have extensive knowledge of this type of property. Depending upon the item, various criteria are used to determine the value of the property. Some things that can be considered include but are not limited to:

- The overall condition of the property:
  - Does it need repairs?
  - The last date of routine maintenance.
- With real estate, location is usually important and "curb appeal" does make a difference.
- Determine the age and authenticity of the item.
- Authenticate the provenance (history) of the collectible.
- Is there a viable market at this time for the item being offered?
- Does the auctioneer have a list of buyers who might be interested in the item?

A savvy auctioneer uses a variety of methods to help evaluate property. His evaluations should be objective, impartial and unbiased and based on knowledge of the item being appraised. It is the responsibility of the auctioneer to determine the value of the item and explain to the seller that the price received at the time of the sale may be higher or lower. Whatever his area of expertise, he should be familiar with and keep up with current trends in the marketplace.

There are publications that specialize in specific items like the blue book that evaluates motor vehicles. Manufacturers usually have published price lists for current products and occasionally have lists for products sold in previous years. The real estate industry has a multi-listing service, MLS, which has information about property in the same area. Courthouse records, which are in the public domain, show the value of similar property. A lot of this information is available online.

An **appraisal** is a written report given to the auctioneer who, depending upon the terms of the Auction Sales Agreement, usually provides a copy to the seller. Some states require the seller receive a copy prior to the sale.

The report should include the following information:

- A complete description of the item.
- Pictures of the item.
- If it is commercial or residential real estate, the exact location and legal description of the property.
- If it is a collectible, the provenance or history.
- The current and potential uses of the property.

- An analysis of the recent selling prices of like items.
- Information about the current activity and market trends for similar items.

The auctioneer should make sure the seller understands that the recent selling price of similar items is only an indication of what the item could sell for. It in no way guarantees the final selling price of the seller's property.

No one can know everything about all the items that could possibly be offered for sale. For that reason alone, it is just a good business practice for an auctioneer to know of and have a list of **experts** in a variety of fields. These people are available to appraise personal and real property and various collectibles and commodities. Some states require a license before a person can perform certified appraisals. These licensed experts often belong to professional organizations with a strict code of ethics, which requires members to abide by and follow a set of industry-approved standard practices.

An expert is a person with a high degree of knowledge about a particular subject. This knowledge can come from a formal education and/or experience in a specialized field of study. An expert is familiar with all aspects of an item including but not limited to its history or provenance, how it was made, its predicted "shelf-life" and common usage, and any architects, builders, manufacturers, artists and previous owners that may have been involved with the item. The expert usually is a member of or affiliated with reputable organizations and groups that can verify his expertise.

Some examples of experts are: real estate agents and brokers, automobile dealers, product manufacturers, art dealers and individual collectors. Experts in collectibles like jewelry, artwork, sculpture or rare books can be found at colleges, universities, libraries and museums.

Appraisers add value to the transaction because they are knowledgeable in their specialized area and offer unbiased, impartial opinions founded on extensive experience. The selling price should reflect the appraised price. It probably won't match the number exactly but it should be close. If it isn't, the auctioneer should find another appraiser.

When interviewing an appraiser, the intention is to learn about his or her expertise in a particular area as well as to determine his or her qualifications and professional affiliations. Some questions that can be asked:

- Are you licensed or certified to practice in the state where the sale is being held?
- Do you have any designated specialties and from which organizations?
- Are you a member of any professional organizations? Which ones?
- How long have you been in practice?
- What experience do you have appraising this type of item?
- How familiar are you with market for these items?

- Explain what methods you use to determine the age and authenticity of these types of items.
- Where did you receive your training in these methods?
- How long have you used these methods? Some of your previous clients?
- May I contact these people for a reference?

Depending upon the appraiser's qualifications and area of expertise, he or she could help with some of the following activities:

- Tax assessment reviews that could affect the sales price.
- Settling estates especially if some or all of the parties live out of the area.
- Issues involving eminent domain and property that could be condemned.
- Resolving divorce, estate, property division, foreclosure and zoning issues.
- Developing data and providing studies concerning supply and demand and market trends.
- Benefits, if any, and cost analysis of making improvements to the property.

It is important to remember that unless the appraiser is also an attorney licensed to practice law in the state in which the property is located, he cannot offer a legal opinion. His function is to evaluate the item and present a written report. If a legal opinion is required, the auctioneer should suggest the client retain legal counsel.

Age, Authenticity and Ownership

Depending upon the item, there are various ways to determine age, authenticity and ownership. Researching the title or deed online or at the city or county courthouse will show previous owners of real estate and give the legal description of the property. In most states, with the vehicle identification number (VIN), the Department of Motor Vehicles can provide the previous owners as well as the year, make and model of the vehicle. Commodities such as jewelry, paintings, sculpture and antiquities sometimes have a provenance or history that can be traced through written records of earlier sales, trades and other transactions. In some situations, special tests, such as carbon dating, can be done to determine the age and/or authenticity.

If the age, authenticity or ownership of the item could be questioned, to protect his reputation, the auctioneer should take whatever steps necessary to remove all doubt.

To avoid any potential problems and/or legal questions, it is imperative to verify the client owns the item being offered and/or has the authority to sell it. If the auctioneer is dealing with an agent, the agent needs to provide documentation authorizing him to act on behalf of the owner of record. If the item is residential or commercial real estate or items such as vehicles or machinery and other commodities, the auctioneer needs to know about any liens or judgments against the property. This information can be found at city and county courthouses. In the case of real estate, the mortgage company can provide financial data. With other items, banks, credit unions and other lending institutions can provide financial data.

To verify ownership of other commodities, previous bills of sale, titles, appraisal reports and wills are some documents that can provide verification of ownership and/or the authority to dispose of the property.

Brokers

A broker is someone who brings sellers and buyers together. The broker does not own or have possession of the item(s) offered for sale. He cannot transfer ownership of the property unless the owner has given him written permission to do so. He may only disclose the name of the owner to the buyer with permission of the owner and usually only after the sale is completed. When the broker informs the buyer who owns the property, the owner is referred to as the disclosed principal.

The broker represents the owner, also known as the principal, in the sales transaction. Sometimes the two parties have a written agreement stating the broker's specific responsibilities, authority and limitations.

Auctioneers

Most experienced auctioneers specialize in a few kinds of auctions. They should advise the seller if the item is appropriate for auction. They should know the value of the item, the type of customers most likely to buy the item and how best to attract those buyers. The auctioneer should know how to advertise effectively and what publications attract motivated buyers. A seller should always ask for and check references. Some states, cities and counties require a license and/or a permit. The seller should make sure these documents are current. Memberships in local, state and national auctioneers associations usually require members keep current with any changes in government regulations and often have a written code of ethics which encourages professionalism. An auctioneer's reputation in the community is invaluable. Trust and respect in their integrity will attract a core of committed buyers. More importantly, these buyers will return to auctions run by these auctioneers.

In order to determine if he can market and sell the property for the best price, the auctioneer should ask the seller:

- How quickly must the item be sold?
- Why does the item need to be sold now?
- Has the client tried selling the item using other methods?
- If so, what methods were used?

While it is the auctioneer's responsibility to determine the market value of the property, the seller should have a general idea of its value before offering the item for sale.

After the initial discussion, the auctioneer and seller decide what services the auctioneer will provide. The contract between the auctioneer and seller lists the specific responsibilities of the auctioneer, his commission, what expenses the seller should expect and when the proceeds of the sale will be distributed. This contract is called the Auction Listing Agreement. Both parties should read and understand the contract before signing.

An auctioneer could give a prospective seller some reasons for offering his property for sale at an auction: to raise cash, clear out clutter, make room for new items. He could explain the specifics of the auction sales agreement and the protections it offers both parties. The auctioneer could discuss the value of advertising and his knowledge of which media promotes the particular property the most effectively. He could describe the excitement of sale day, how the items are presented and the energy generated by motivated buyers, which can increase the sale price. He could offer assurances that the financial details will be handled with honesty, accuracy and the disbursement of funds will be made as quickly as practical. Whatever information the auctioneer provides will help the seller made an educated decision as to whether this is the best method to dispose of his property.

An auctioneer could describe the excitement of sale day to a prospective buyer. He could inform the buyer that frequently the fair market value of an item is determined through the auction process. The auctioneer could describe the items being offered at a particular auction so the buyer can decide if he is interested in participating. He could offer the catalogue for the buyer to read and study for details about the items being offered. Since auctions can be cancelled, he could suggest the buyer call the day of the sale to make sure the sale is on. He could discuss the energy of the bidding process and recommend the buyer have a clear idea of how much he believes the item is worth and the top price he is willing to pay. Whatever information the auctioneer provides will help the buyer make an education decision about whether to participate at this auction or wait until a more appropriate sale.

Sometimes no matter how good the presentation and competitive the prices, the prospective client decides not to sell the property, or worse, hires another auctioneer. There is no guaranteed way to avoid losing a client but there are some signs to watch for. Make sure the person is really ready to sell. If he or she wants to think about it for a couple of days, needs to talk to family members or uses some other stalling tactic, say thank you and leave. If the auctioneer persists, he could appear "pushy" and a "hard sell" which could offend some people.

If the prospective client indicates he will call later to make arrangements for the sale and then signs with someone else, there is another problem: the original auctioneer neglected to contact the seller in a day or two to finalize the agreement. Do not lose a sale waiting for a return call. Always follow up.

Auctioneer's License

The auctioneer's license is proof the holder has attended a state approved auctioneer's school and passed the state required written examination. In most states without that license, a person cannot legally conduct an auction (with some exceptions). The license must be displayed while calling bids and carried while conducting any auction-related business. For these reasons, most states issue both a certificate that can be framed and a pocket-sized copy for the wallet. The auctioneer's name, license number and expiration date are shown on both versions. The license must be available for inspection during a sale or while conducting business as an auctioneer. A designated agent of the state licensing bureau, the seller and buyer may review the license during any auction-related activities.

Some states do not require an auctioneer's license but many require a business license or permit to operate in their jurisdiction. It is the auctioneer's responsibility to make sure he complies with all state and local requirements.

Several states require that an auctioneer be certified and/or licensed in order to call bids at an auction. Licensing requirements may differ from state to state but most generally require the candidate:

- Be at least eighteen years of age
- Has not, within the last five years:
    - Pleaded guilty to a felony.
    - Entered a plea of nolo contendere to a felony.
    - Committed or been convicted of fraud or moral turpitude.
    - Committed any act that could be grounds for suspension or revocation of his license.
- Had his auctioneer's license revoked for any reason.
- Attended and completed a state approved auctioneering school program.
- Complete a specific number of classroom hours of instruction.
- Pass a state sponsored written examination.

Once the auctioneer has his license, many states require a certain number of state-approved continuing professional education hours every year in order to renew the license.

Most states requiring a licensed auctioneer to conduct auctions allow these exceptions to the rule:

- Sales conducted by the owner of the goods - as long as the purpose is not to resell items.
- Sales by an owner's agent - as long as the agent is not an auctioneer (for example, the owner's attorney).
- Sales by a federal, state or local government agency.
- Sales by order of a United States Bankruptcy Court.
- Sales of livestock authorized by the Commissioner of Agriculture.
- Sales by and/or for a recognized charitable organization.
- One annual sale by and/or for a civic group.
- Sales of real property by a trustee.

This list by no means includes every exception allowed by every state. In order to avoid violating any state statutes, it is prudent to contact the state's licensing bureau before planning and/or holding any type of auction.

Reputation

The most important feature of a successful auctioneer is his or her reputation. Once an ethical reputation is established, it is much easier to market services and attract willing sellers and qualified buyers. One thing to always remember when approaching potential clients and insuring qualified buyers return is that people buy from people. They don't buy from companies or because of a list of services. All discussions concerning services and rates and policies and procedures should be open, clearly stated and legal. A key ingredient in building and maintaining a solid reputation is to respect the competition and never talk negatively about a competitor. If the auctioneer conducts every aspect of the auction process from the first conversation through the distribution of the proceeds fairly and with a minimum of problems and complications for the seller and the buyer, he will build a successful business and establish a solid reputation.

Code of Conduct

There is a written code of conduct auctioneers are expected to follow. The wording in each state's code may be different but the intent is the same. This code must be honored or the auctioneer could risk suspension or revocation of his license. Some areas included but certainly not limited to:

- Obligations to the seller:
    - Contract prepared with description of item(s) being offered.
    - Date for the sale.
    - Advertising plan and budget prepared and presented for approval.
    - Owner kept informed about all aspects of the sale process.
    - Detailed settlement statement provided.
    - Distribution of proceeds completed in a timely manner.
    - Reserve price not disclosed without prior permission of seller.
- Obligations to the buyer:
    - Adequate time to inspect offered items.
    - Knowledge and understanding of all sale items.
    - Payment options clearly stated and honored at the sale.
    - Prompt release of goods upon full payment or as stated in the bill of sale.

The auctioneer also has an obligation to the general public that the information in all advertising media is true, accurate and complete to best of his knowledge. He should verify ownership and the authority of the person to sell the item(s) as well as the authenticity of every item offered. He should make sure all items are ready for inspection on the day(s) and at the time(s) promised. All relevant documents should be available for review, i.e. titles, appraisals, health certificates, maintenance records, etc. He should guarantee all items advertised are available on the day of the sale or post notices if an item has been withdrawn. He should open the sale site on the date and at the time advertised.

The auctioneer should conduct himself with honesty, integrity and professionalism while performing all duties and actions involved in the auction process. From the initial meeting with the client to the settlement statement presented after the sale to delivery of the goods to the buyer, he should honor and respect the auctioneer's code of conduct.

Visibility and Advertising

Business cards should always show the auctioneer's name and office and cell phone numbers. Other information that can be included: the auction company's name, physical and mailing addresses (if different), an email address and web site information (if applicable). Other literature, whether it is a brochure, one-page flyer or a web site, can list professional affiliations, awards received, specialized knowledge or experience and services and prices. It can also define common auction terms and answer frequently asked questions. The more information provided to the potential client, the more informed the decision and the fewer potential problems.

Since it is a silent salesperson, all marketing material should present a professional image, be clean, uncluttered, easy to read and understand, address common issues and answer questions. The auctioneer should always remember that he or she only has one chance to make a first impression and once made, that impression is difficult to change.

Joining social, volunteer and professional organizations, offering to serve on boards of directors and becoming a member of various committees is a very **visible** way to become known in the community. Giving talks and presentations at schools, churches, civic clubs, business groups and senior centers also provides a way to promote the auctioneer's name and services to diverse audiences. The auctioneer needs to network constantly to develop lists of potential sellers and buyers. A successful strategy is to make some kind of contact with people in his database every six months. The communication can be a newsletter, a holiday greeting, a personal note or a notice about seminars and presentations. Writing interesting, informative articles for the local paper and trade publications is another method to establish a reputation. The important thing is the auctioneer needs to keep his name in the public conscience.

In order for a potential client to make an educated decision about what kind of auction to use and which auctioneer and/or auction company to hire, the seller needs to understand the entire process from the appraisal of the item for sale before the auction to the distribution of the proceeds after the auction. It is to the auctioneer's benefit to present the information clearly and answer all the client's questions honestly and directly.

Important information the auctioneer should include in all **marketing material**: the types of auctions available and his experience with each one, who will pay what expenses and when, and the services available and fees charged. All policies and procedures need to be addressed so the seller knows what to expect every step of the way. Fees and what services they represent should be clearly stated and explained so there are no misunderstanding later.

Potential clients with possible sale items include but are not limited to: civic and charitable organizations; retail, warehouse and service-related businesses and government agencies with new, refurbished, rebuilt and excess inventory. Lists of these organizations and business can be found in the Yellow Pages and at the public library. The auctioneer can call to discuss his services, make an appointment or stop by and leave marketing material to be read later. Whatever contact method is used, it is important to speak to the decision maker.

Public sources of information are tax and property records available at city halls and the county courthouses and, in some cities and counties, online. Legal notices are published in some trade journals and industry newsletters and local newspapers. Developing a network of estate planning attorneys is another source of potential business for the enterprising auctioneer. These specialized attorneys will sometimes be responsible for disposing of a client's entire estate.

There are many ways to **advertise**. Besides networking person-to-person and in person-to-group environments and developing informative marketing materials to hand out personally, various other media is available. Ads in the Yellow Pages are very effective. People still turn to the phone book to look for service providers in specialties with which they are unfamiliar. These ads are available twenty-four hours a day, seven days a week, three hundred sixty-five days a year and they never take a vacation. Radio and television advertising can be effective but is usually expensive. Newspaper, magazine and trade journal ads and direct mail pieces are other ways to reach potential clients but must be repeated regularly to be effective.

The auctioneer should use a variety of advertising media. It is important to understand the target audience so advertising reaches the intended demographic. All advertising methods and marketing material used needs to be carefully tracked to determine its effectiveness.

It is important to discuss the advertising plan with the client (seller). It is the auctioneer's responsibility to decide what media will be the most effective method in reaching the target audience. He needs to explain what type of media is available, which is the most effective for this particular auction, how many times and at what intervals the chosen media will be used and what each will cost.

Radio, television, newspaper, direct mail pieces and billboard advertising is expensive but can be effective if repeated enough times to make an impression on the target buyers. Flyers announcing the auction, placed in strategic locations several times before the sale, are a low cost means of getting the word out. The brochure printed prior to the auction that includes all the items scheduled for sale at the same auction is a cost effective way to showcase the individual sellers' items.

Effective advertising can make or break a sale. Advertising is expensive, some media more than others so if the campaign is not planned in detail, well-written and produced in a professional manner, the impact will be negative and a waste of the client's money. The first rule of any advertising campaign is to always respect the target audience, never talk down to them and never insult their intelligence with wild promises and ridiculous claims. The astute consumer will see the message for what it is and isn't anyway. The auctioneer should strive to develop a reputation for accurate, factual advertising. This will make it easier to attract clients and keep qualified buyers coming back. A potential seller or buyer may not need the auctioneer's services at the time he sees, hears or reads the advertising piece, but if the message is clear and concise, it will be remembered when services are needed.

Since most people respond to visual stimuli, pictures are extremely effective in any kind of advertising media (radio is the exception). Pictures and drawings convey a lot without requiring the viewer do much work. The contents of the description will vary depending upon the item. For example, residential and commercial real estate will include the location while commodities such as jewelry and art should mention the designer or artist. Advertising should always include who is holding the sale, the day, date and time, the location of the sale and any special requirements. For example, is pre-registration required, what methods of payment are accepted, etc.

It is important to make sure all the laws of the state and the rules and regulations of the Federal Trade Commission (FTC) are followed in all advertising media. Some cities and counties also have strict ordinances stipulating the size, location and content of billboards and other roadside signs.

Newspaper ads and **billboards** have only about three seconds to grab the reader's attention so it is vital the main message stands out. This is why pictures are very effective in this type of advertising. The layout should be uncluttered and come to the point quickly. This type of media requires the information be presented in large, easy to read font with clear, understandable graphics. The headline needs to either entice or inform so the reader keeps reading. Newspaper ads are competing with other information on the page so getting the reader's attention is vital. The copy should answer who, what, where, when questions. Unless the reader is stuck in traffic, billboards must literally be read on the run so the fewer words used, the better. But the words still need to answer who, what, where, when questions. Both newspaper ads and billboards should list a phone number for additional information.

If **radio** and/or **television** are part of the advertising campaign, a script must be prepared and actors hired to read the parts. The auctioneer can take a role in the production by reading the copy for the radio spot or acting in the television commercial. Whoever reads the script must be a professional; amateurs can often unintentionally ruin a well-written, effective script.

This type of media is expensive so it is important to consider the target buyers' listening and viewing habits when scheduling the days and times the commercials air. The best source for this information is the auctioneer's experience combined with demographic reports available from the radio and television stations. After using radio and television media a few times, the auctioneer should have a better understanding for the best time of the day to reach the target buyer.

One of the things a good auctioneer acquires while networking is names of people and what kind of items they might be interested in bidding on at auction. These lists provide valuable contacts. Once a **direct mail** piece has been sent, it is important to follow up with a **phone call** within a couple of days. This accomplishes several objectives: it confirms receipt of the direct mail piece, gives the auctioneer the opportunity to personally invite the buyer to the sale and learn if he is planning to attend the event and offers the potential buyer the chance to ask any questions. The auctioneer can eliminate the initial direct mail contact and call the potential buyer instead. This method works best with buyers who have attended previous auctions and/or have requested a courtesy call about upcoming sales and with people the auctioneer has already established a business relationship.

The first requirement for **flyers**, **direct mail** pieces and **brochures** to be effective is well-written words delivered in an attractive format that is easy to read. Poorly written and inadequately proofed copy presented in an unprofessional manner will leave a negative impression and the main message may be missed. Hiring professionals to design, write and produce written advertising pieces is a good way to insure a quality product that gets the right kind of attention and doesn't end up in the wastebasket

Direct mail pieces are invitations, letters and post cards sent to a targeted list of potential buyers. To be truly effective, more than one direct mail piece should be sent at designated intervals. Flyers are an effective and economic method to promote the auction. A brochure offers more space to discuss the items for sale. The descriptions can be more detailed and better pictures can be used.

In order to learn the effectiveness of the advertising campaign, it is critical to track the response to the media used. The auctioneer should keep a calendar showing how often radio and television ads aired, how many direct mail pieces were mailed, when and to whom, the number of brochures given out at which events and how often the web site is visited after notification of a sale is posted. As buyers register for the auction, ask how they heard about the sale and note the answer on a checklist. After the sale, analyze the data collected to determine how effective each type of media was for this particular sale. Over time, the auctioneer will accumulate useful information and develop a solid understanding of how effective each type of media is in attracting target buyers for every type of auction. Including this data in presentations may help convince prospective clients to sign a contract for future auctions.

To be competitive in today's market, it is important to have a presence on the **World Wide Web**. Like all good advertising, the web site should reflect the culture of the company and the integrity of the owners and staff. The site should have accurate, timely information, be easy to navigate and list phone and fax numbers and email addresses. Facts about the company and its history, frequently asked questions about auction procedures and legal requirements and professional biographies of key people are areas to include. Pictures of busy auction sites and previously sold items along with positive seller and buyer comments are other things to consider. Providing a copy of the Auction Sales Agreement and other forms used would be helpful and instructive. Listing upcoming sales with the accompanying brochure that can be downloaded is a very effective promotional tool. For maximum impact, it is a good idea to have a professional design and maintain the site.

No matter what media is used, there are basic elements that need to be addressed and criteria met to create an effective advertising campaign. These include but are not limited to:

- Develop a realistic budget and stick to it.
- Plan a campaign that reflects the items being offered.
- Know the target audience and what motivates them.
- Choose the advertising media that appeals to that target group.
- Use professionals to create the marketing pieces.
- Have at least three people proof all material for spelling, grammar and content.
- Use accurate facts, figures, pictures and other miscellaneous data.
- Be sure to include who, where, when, what and any special requirements of the sale.
- Always follow all FTC rules and regulations and state and local requirements.
- Analyze data about effectiveness of media used.

Auction Contracts

The Auction Contract, also called the Auction Sales Agreement, is a legal document listing what services the auctioneer will provide, what fees will be charged and the seller's responsibilities. The document includes:

- The name of the state and county in which the auction will be held.
- The date the contract was entered into and signed.
- An acknowledgement the seller agrees to employ the auctioneer.
- The date and time the sale (auction) will be held.
- A detailed description of the property offered for sale.
- An agreement the seller will provide a good title to the buyers.
- What specific services the auctioneer will provide.
- A list of people who will be paid for their participation.
- A statement specifying the commission to be paid to the auctioneer by the seller.
- Any other terms and conditions as needed.

The auctioneer retains the original document. The seller receives a duplicate copy.

PROPOSALS

Sometimes a prospective client will request a written proposal before making a decision about offering his property at auction and/or hiring a particular auctioneer or auction company. The proposal should cover all aspects of the process including but not limited to:

- Basic information about the kind of auction recommended for the item being offered for sale.
- A proposed budget with specific expenses, including staff required and miscellaneous services available, explained and costs estimated.
- A general discussion of the marketing process and the potential buyers being targeted.
- A timetable that includes when the appraisal will occur, how long the advertising will last, a proposed date for the actual sale and when to expect distribution of the proceeds.
- A detailed list of all available services with their fees.
- A section with frequently asked general questions would be helpful.

The proposal should be presented in a professional, clear, concise format on good quality paper.

The seller needs to understand each step in the auction process and every procedure involved. All available services should be explained in detail and fees quoted before the seller accepts any service. An advertising plan targeted toward interested buyers should be discussed and a realistic budget developed and agreed to by both the auctioneer and the seller. The auctioneer should explain what personnel are needed to prepare for and conduct the sale. Their duties should be clearly defined. All miscellaneous expenses (for example: set up and tear down of the sale site, refreshments if offered, etc.) should be discussed and cost estimates provided. The auctioneer's fee and what it covers needs to be discussed and agreed upon. How and when the proceeds of the sale will be distributed should be explained in detail. The seller should provide an accurate description of the item for sale.

INVENTORY

An inventory is an itemized list of all the items included in the Auction Listing Agreement. It is important to have a detailed description of every item so there is no confusion about which item is being offered. This is especially critical if the seller owns duplicates or similar items and is only placing one for sale. In order to avoid the possibility of questions during the auction itself or after the sale is concluded, a complete and accurate inventory should be taken prior to the sale. The seller and the auctioneer should sign the inventory record verifying its accuracy. If there is any possibility of ownership issues or questions about the authenticity of any item on the inventory, it would be helpful if the signatures on the inventory record are witnessed. Having a Notary Public present at the signing to validate the signatures may be required in some states.

A comprehensive inventory should include, but is not limited to, the following information:

- Detailed description of each item. The description will vary depending upon the individual item. If similar items are in the sale, describe each one. If this is not possible, find a common description for the entire lot.
- Pictures, drawings, schematics.
- For the following items include:
  - Real estate: location and legal description, condition of any buildings.
  - Machinery: make, model and serial number.
  - Jewelry: caret, color and weight, designer (if known).
  - Paintings and Sculptures: artist, year/period created and provenance.
  - Other commodities vary depending upon the item.
  - Vehicles: make, model and vehicle identification number (VIN).
  - Livestock: breed, gender, age.
- If appropriate, maintenance records and/or appraisal reports.

Once the inventory is completed, assign a lot number to each item or group of items and record the lot number on the inventory record.

BEFORE THE SALE

Sale Sites: The size and location of the sale site will depend on what items are being auctioned and the number of people expected to attend. If the auctioneer is on the staff of an auction company, the company may own or lease one or several locations. If the property being offered for sale is residential or commercial real estate, personal property such as jewelry and collectibles, paintings, sculptures and rare wines, etc., the sale could be held in an auditorium or hall. If motor vehicles, large machinery or livestock is being auctioned, a more appropriate outdoor arena is necessary. Local ordinances may also regulate the location and how large the site needs to be for a particular type of auction. It is important for the auctioneer to be aware of and follow all regulations from securing permits to complying with load capacity stipulations to addressing potential traffic problems and parking issues.

It may be necessary for the auctioneer to arrange for people to set up chairs, tables, and a podium and make other additions or alterations in the auditorium, hall or outside arena to accommodate sale items and the anticipated crowd. He may need to contract for and arrange set up of the sound equipment including the microphone and public address system. It may be necessary to arrange for rest room facilities and port-a-potties. In certain jurisdictions, some workers may be members of various unions. The auctioneer needs to be aware of, understand and respect all union contracts.

If food and/or beverages are to be provided free or for a nominal charge, the auctioneer needs to arrange for caterers, wait staff and bartenders. If plans call for alcohol to be served, it would also be prudent to verify if it is permissible to serve alcohol in this location and/or if a special permit is required at this type of event.

Documentation: Depending upon the residential or commercial property, the type of machinery, motor vehicle, business equipment, commodity and/or personal property to be offered at the auction, certain legal documents may need to be agreed upon, drafted and signed prior to the day of the sale. These documents can include, but are not limited to, permits, licenses, agreements, contracts, appraisal reports, certified financial statements and other fiduciary data as well as miscellaneous state, county and municipal forms. This documentation may vary from state to state, county to county and city to city. The completion of a sale could be jeopardized if one of these paperwork requirements is overlooked, completed incorrectly or fraudulently executed. It is the auctioneer's responsibility to know, understand and comply with all the laws, rules and regulations and complete all necessary paperwork in a timely fashion in the states, cities and counties in which he or she is licensed.

Sale items: Even if it is an "as is" auction, making a few minor improvements always enhances the salability of an item. If residential or commercial property is being offered, the grass should be cut, the bushes trimmed and, in appropriate weather, the snow removed. Buildings and other structures should be repaired, cleaned and, if necessary, painted inside and/or out. Routine maintenance should be performed on motor vehicles, large and small machinery and office equipment (copy machines, printers, computers, fax machines, telephone systems, etc.) prior to the sale. Small personal items should have minor repairs done and, where appropriate, be cleaned and polished. A veterinarian should see livestock and the animals should be tested for diseases. Other commodities should be packed, crated or bundled appropriately.

If necessary, the auctioneer should arrange appropriate transportation to the sale site. If not sold, the item needs to be returned. This service is usually charged to the seller.

Other duties: After inspecting the property, the auctioneer may suggest things the seller should do to prepare the property before day of the sale. For example if selling real estate, the seller could paint the inside and/or outside of the house or commercial building, clean the windows inside and out, mow the grass and trim the bushes and remove any clutter that detracts from the look of the property. Other commodities could be cleaned and have routine maintenance done.

Prior to sale day, the auctioneer will market the property. There are several methods that may be used: print, radio, television and Internet advertising. He may also design a brochure, send out direct mail pieces and post flyers in strategic locations that target potential buyers.

The auctioneer will also decide which type of auction would attract the most motivated buyers and generate the highest price for the property, which is the ultimate goal for both seller and auctioneer.

Sale Day

The auctioneer will clean and set up the auction area. He will organize and display the items for sale. He will catalogue and tag all items with lot numbers. He will answer questions prior to the start of the bidding. He will register potential buyers by collecting names, addresses, phone numbers and driver's license numbers. Once the auction begins, he will call the bids, collect the money and close the sale.

Money collected the day of the sale is usually deposited in an escrow account. Distribution of the proceeds is based on the terms spelled out in the Auction Listing Agreement. The seller pays all expenses, which are deducted from the gross proceeds. Expenses include but are not limited to advertising and printing costs and rental, catering and staff fees. The auctioneer's commission, usually a pre-determined percentage of the gross proceeds, is also deducted. The remaining funds are given to the seller.

Bidder Cards

The auctioneer supplies bidder cards (or paddles). A bidder card is three inches by five inches (3" x 5") and made of heavy card stock in a bright, bold color that is easy to spot. The cards can be ordered blank or pre-numbered. Cards sometimes have the auction terms and conditions printed on the back. They are used to note the items the buyer successfully bid on and are given to the cashier by the bidder to match to the clerking ticket sheet. A card is given to each bidder after he registers. The card has the bidder number printed or written on it in big, bold script so the auctioneer and ring personnel can read the number from a distance. This number is entered on the registration list with the buyer's name, address, phone number and driver's license number. This assigned bidder number is written on all auction paperwork, including checks and credit card receipts.

Terms and conditions that could be listed on the back of the bidder card:

- Buyers/agents must register before bidding.
- By accepting and using this card, bidder acknowledges he has read, understands and agrees to all terms and conditions listed.
- Should there be a dispute between bidders, the auctioneer's decision is final.
- Payment is due the day of the sale.
- Highest bidder owns the item.
- Once the item is sold, neither auctioneer nor staff is responsible for theft of or damage to the item.
- Auctioneer has the right to reject any bid.
- Auctioneer has the right to combine, divide or withdraw lots from the auction.
- All items are sold "where is, as is" with no warranty stated or implied.
- All sales are final.
- Attendees are responsible for the safety of their family, employees and guests.

The Clerk

During the auction, the clerk keeps track of what item is sold to which bidder. He is responsible for recording specific information on the clerking ticket sheet. This includes:

- A brief description of the item sold.
- The lot number of the item.
- The buyer's bidder number.
- The number of items sold to the bidder.
- The amount to be paid for the item.

If there are two items for sale, sometimes the bidder is allowed to take their choice. If this is the case, the clerk indicates which item the buyer purchased on the clerking ticket sheet.

A clerking ticket sheet is a three-part form used to keep track of which items are sold during the auction. These sheets have spaces for twelve (12) items. As each item is presented to the audience for consideration, the clerk records the lot number and a brief description. When the item has been sold, the clerk adds the bidder number and the purchase price. When the entire sheet has been filled in, it is given to the cashier. It is the cashier's responsibility to complete any calculations and match the bidder cards to the completed clerking ticket sheets. Sometimes a buyer will want to pay for his purchases before the end of the auction. If so, it may be necessary to explain the clerking ticket sheet has not reached the cashier and it may take a few minutes to complete the sheet.

Settlement Statements

The settlement statement is the document prepared by the cashier from the information on the various clerking ticket sheets that lists all the items purchased by one buyer. The statement shows the bidder number, the lot numbers, a brief description of each item and the winning bids. The cashier totals the numbers and attaches the calculator tape to the statement. The cashier reviews the settlement statement with the auctioneer to verify that all items purchased are listed at the correct price. The auctioneer and/or the cashier review the information on the settlement statement with the buyer. Full and complete payment is required on the day of the sale. At most auctions, payment can be made by cash, check or credit card. If the buyer has provided a letter of guarantee from his financial institution, the cashier verifies the amount specified in this document.

Cashier Responsibilities

The cashier performs several important functions before, during and after the auction. Before the auction:

- Generates the bidder's registration sheet, which lists the bidder number and name, address, phone number and driver's license numbers of the bidder.
- If required, holds a deposit or letter of guarantee from all registered bidder's financial institutions.

During the auction: Tallies clerking ticket sheets and completes necessary calculations.

- Totals the buyer's items, accepts payment, gives bidder copy of his clerking tickets.

After the auction: Tallies all clerking tickets sheets.

- Totals all moneys received including cash, checks and credit card charges.
- Deducts petty cash to determine gross proceeds of the sale.
- Gross proceeds figure should equal the total of all clerking ticket sheets.
- Deducts all expenses from gross proceeds to determine net proceeds.
- Prepares the Settlement Statement.
- Reviews the Settlement Statement with the auctioneer and the seller.

Ring Personnel

A smart auctioneer appreciates the role of ring personnel or the people who help keep the pace of the auction moving. Depending upon the number of items being offered for sale, there are usually five, six or seven ring people. Some auctioneers require ring personnel to wear the same shirt. This presents a professional image and makes it easy for the auctioneer and the bidders to identify them in the crowd. These folks need to be friendly, able to answers questions about the items being offered for sale and willing to encourage potential buyers to bid. Ring personnel contribute to the auction by helping buyers feel relaxed and comfortable which helps keep the bidding momentum going.

The ring man is the person who is most knowledgeable about the items being offered for sale. He prepares a plan that shows the order in which each item will be presented for bid and at what time.

Auctioneer Chant

There are different names given to the auctioneer's chant. Some of the most common descriptions are: calling bids, crying bids or chanting. They all mean the same thing and can be and are used interchangeably. The chant is the unique mixture of numbers and filler words developed by each auctioneer to encourage buyers to bid on the items offered for sale. The most important aspect of the chant is that the bidders must be able to understand what the auctioneer is saying. If he speaks so fast the words, or more importantly, the numbers, become unintelligible, buyers may become confused and stop bidding. To prevent this from happening, the auctioneer must concentrate on enunciating every word and number clearly so there is no confusion or misunderstanding. Being understood is much more important that being speedy. The goal is a chanting style that is pleasing to the ear, keeps the bidders engaged and the bidding flowing smoothly.

The main purpose for learning and practicing **tongue twisters** is to loosen the face, lips and vocal cords. Even seasoned auctioneers stretch these muscles before calling bids to avoid straining their voices. With practice, the auctioneer will increase his speed but should always remember to focus on pronouncing the words clearly so he is understood by and doesn't confuse the bidders.

Common tongue twisters include:

- Rubber baby buggy bumpers.
- Silly Sally sells seashells by the seashore.
- Round the rugged rock the ragged rascal ran.

(Repeat three times each)

The auctioneer should practice the first three rhymes before trying this one:

- Betty Botter bought some butter, but she said, "This butter's bitter. If I put it in my batter, it will make my batter bitter." So Sally bought a bit of better butter and put it in her bitter batter and it made her bitter batter better.

A new auctioneer makes mistakes, can forget the last bid and gets tongue-tied while developing his unique chanting style. One way to minimize the errors and reduce the nervousness and anxiety during the first few attempts at calling bids is to practice, practice, practice. Like any new activity, it takes time to learn how to sound like the auctioneers who have been perfecting their craft for years. It is permissible to copy someone in the beginning but the goal of every auctioneer is to develop a chanting style all his own. It is always better to be an original than a copy.

A new auctioneer needs to develop a comfortable monotone hum. It will help maintain a steady rhythm as he practices various tongue twisters. He may change the hum as he gets more proficient at bid calling but this drone hum is essential to producing an effective, easy to understand chant.

Filler words can be a single word or a short phrase. These words or expressions are used in between the bid already made and the bid the auctioneer wants to encourage from the buyers. The quicker an item is sold, the fewer filler words the auctioneer will need to use. Filler words should make sense and improve the bid calling by contributing to the rhythm and flow of the chant. With practice and experience, the auctioneer develops a set of filler words with which he is comfortable and that enhance his unique chanting style.

Here is a partial list of common filler words and phrases:

- Now
- Now go
- Now bid
- I've got
- I'm bid
- I want
- Will you give
- Will you bid

- Will you go
- Go
- Want
- Need
- Kick it off
- What am I bid
- Who'll buy 'em at
- Who'll give
- Who'll bid
- Who'll

Number Drills

The most important part of the chant is learning to say the numbers clearly so the buyers understand what the current bid is and what bid is expected next. The auctioneer can use the words quarter, half and seventy-five to break the monotony of using all numbers. Using these words also changes the flow of the chant a bit and gives the listeners a little nudge to help prevent their attention from wondering. It keeps the bidders engaged and involved in the bidding process. Once the bid reaches into the hundreds, it is important to state amounts in such a way the buyers know they are not bidding in single dollar increments. For example: one ten, one twenty, two thirty, two forty, etc. The objective is to sell the item for the highest possible price, not to confuse potential buyers.

Qualifying Potential Buyers

Because of the monetary and/or appraised value of the property, collectibles or commodities being offered for sale at certain auctions, the auctioneer should verify potential buyers' financial information. This qualification also prevents the possibility of not being able to complete a sale because the winning bidder does not have adequate funds to pay for the item. There are several ways to verify financial solvency. Requiring buyers to present a certified letter of credit from their financial institution and calling the bank to verify its authenticity is often a prerequisite for registering as a bidder. Another method is to have the clerk do a credit check with one or all three of the major credit bureaus. Equifax, Experian and Trans Union can be accessed via the Internet and establishing an account with these companies is relatively easy. Verifying credit information to avoid potential problems with a sale is well worth the cost involved.

Encouraging Bidding

When the item is presented for sale, the auctioneer and/or the ring man should show the item and describe how to use it. If the item is a machine or other piece of equipment, demonstrate its function by starting it or moving the parts. For collectibles, he can praise its beauty and usefulness and mention the author, artist, architect or designer. It is the auctioneer's responsibility to convince potential buyers it is to their advantage to own whatever item is being offered for sale.

It is the potential buyer's responsibility to read the catalogue, know what is being offered and have questions answered prior to the sale. It is inappropriate and disruptive to make inquiries during the actual bidding process. It is the auctioneer's responsibility to ensure potential buyers have ample opportunity to inspect the items and ask questions before the sale starts.

Bidding Responsibilities

Ring personnel bring the items to the stage or front of the arena. If it is a commercial or residential real estate auction, pictures and diagrams can be used. Ring personnel also encourage bidding and help keep the sale moving smoothly. The clerk completes the clerking ticket sheets and arranges to get them to the cashier in a timely manner. The cashier tallies clerking ticket sheets and accepts payments.

The auctioneer announces the type of bid being accepted as each item is presented, spots the bidders, calls the bids correctly, sets the pace of the auction and controls the enthusiasm of the crowd. He needs to be able to do simple addition in his head quickly and accurately. The auctioneer also needs to know when a person is bidding and when he's scratching his nose. In other words, he needs to read his audience to avoid missing a bid or misinterpreting a movement.

It is the auctioneer's responsibility to determine who made the winning bid. His decision is final. He needs to be aware of any and all telephone and online bids made before and during the auction and absentee bids received prior to the sale. Acceptance or rejection of all bids is determined by the rules of the auction company as well as any special considerations concerning a particular sale. Some states, cities and counties have statues and ordinances stipulating how certain bids must be handled. The auctioneer needs to be aware of and follow all government regulations. There should never be any questions about what kind or how bids are accepted and processed.

No matter what type of bids are used, it is the buyer's responsibility to know and understand the parameters and requirements prior to the sale. This information can be obtained by calling the auction company or visiting their web site.

Opening Announcements

Before the bidding starts, the auctioneer makes opening announcements about the requirements of this particular sale. He should remind the bidders they must register before bidding by completing a buyer's form; they need to have a bidder number assigned and recorded by the cashier; and they need a bidder's card or paddle to be recognized by the auctioneer and the ring personnel during the bidding process. He could also remind the buyers that if they have a letter of credit, it must be given to the cashier so it can be verified prior to the start of the bidding.

It is prudent for the auctioneer to arrange to have the opening announcements either taped recorded or video taped. This precaution provides a permanent record of what was said and eliminates the possibility of questions about the rules of the auction company and the requirements of this particular sale once the auction is over.

Other Bidding Types

A **tie bid** occurs when two or more buyers offer the identical price for the same item. This can happen when telephone, online and absentee bids are accepted.

A **late bid** occurs after the bidding has been closed.

A **telephone bid** is made via an open telephone line during the auction. A specific phone line is dedicated to receive these bids.

An **online bid** is made via the Internet during the auction. A special link is established to receive these bids.

An **absentee bid** is a written offer made prior to the auction. It is usually received before the day of the sale. The deadline varies but is generally close of business the day before the sale date.

Telephone, Online and Absentee Bids

If a buyer wants to bid via telephone or online, he must register prior to the day of the auction. He must complete a bidder's form. Information includes but is not limited to: sale date, name, address, phone and fax numbers, email address, credit card name, number and expiration date plus a shipping address if different. The buyer lists the lot number and a brief description of the item or items on which he is planning to bid.

The bidder's registration form must be received before the day of the sale. The deadline varies depending upon the items being sold and the rules of the auction company and/or auctioneer. Sometimes a minimum bid is required in order to bid by telephone or online. These rules are often stated in the auction catalogue. Buyers can also get this information by calling the auction company or visiting their web site.

The credit card information required to register telephone, online and absentee bidders is used for verification purposes only. If the telephone or online bidder makes the winning bid, he is asked how payment will be made. If the buyer wants to charge his purchase, he gives the cashier permission to process the charge with the credit card company. In most situations, if he wants to pay by cash or check, he must present payment within twenty-four hours.

A buyer unable to attend the auction in person can use an absentee bid. This written bid must include sale date, name, address, phone and fax numbers, email address, credit card information and shipping address. The bid lists the lot number, which must match the auction catalogue, a brief description of the item or items and the highest price he is willing to pay for each item.

In most cases, the absentee bid must be received before the sale, usually by close of business the day before. Occasionally the auctioneer will accept bids up to sixty (60) minutes before the start of the sale. Because of the activity on sale day and to avoid the risk of the bid being misplaced or ignored, it is better to have the bid delivered prior to the day of the sale. The buyer should contact the auction company to verify the bid was received.

If an absentee bidder is the successful bidder, in most cases, he is notified within twenty-four hours. He is offered the opportunity to pay by credit card and authorizes the charge at that time. If he prefers to pay by cash or check, he must arrange payment within twenty-four hours. Most auctioneers and auction companies do not offer a COD (cash on delivery) option. The auctioneer needs to be familiar with any state and/or local government regulations concerning these payments.

Puffing

Puffing is a term used to describe a person representing the seller whose only reason for attending the auction is to inflate the price of the item being offered for sale. These individuals are called puffers or by-bidders. They have no intention of purchasing any item for themselves, family members or anyone else. They are at the auction at the request of the seller and act as the seller's agent. The puffer usually enters into a secret understanding with the seller to make fictitious bids for the sole purpose of driving up the selling price of the owner's property. In most states, the by-bidder is not legally liable for his actions because he has entered into a contractual agreement with the seller to perform a service.

Complete Sales

A sale is done when the auctioneer declares the item sold and the sale complete. Most auctioneers use a gavel or have a particular hand motion that indicates the sale is done. Until he makes a statement like "sold for $120 to bidder number 145" and brings the gavel down, the sale is still open and the bidding continues.

If a bid is made at the same moment the gavel goes down, at his discretion, the auctioneer can either declare the sale completed or he can reopen the bidding. If he reopens the bidding, it does not mean the last bidder automatically bought the item. All reopening the bidding means is the auctioneer has recognized the last bid and agreed to continue the bidding. The auctioneer should always keep in mind that his goal to sell every item at the highest possible price.

Withdrawing Items

In a reserve auction (a minimum bid has been set by the seller), the auctioneer may withdraw the item being offered for sale at any time before or after the bidding begins as long as he announces the decision before he declares the item has been sold and the sale completed. In an auction without reserve (there is no minimum bid set before the sale), the auctioneer cannot withdraw an item from the sale once he calls for the bidding to begin. The only exception to this rule is if there is no bid made within a prescribed amount of time. This time limit is established before the sale begins and is usually part of the routine rules and regulations published by the auction company and/or set forth by the auctioneer.

WITHDRAWING BIDS

A buyer can withdraw his bid at any time before the auctioneer declares the item sold and the sale complete. This rule applies in most states and it doesn't matter whether the auction is a reserve or without reserve sale. If the buyer withdraws his bid, this does not mean the previously offered bid is active. At this point, it is the decision of the auctioneer whether to reopen the bidding or to withdraw the item from the sale.

If the auctioneer has not informed the bidders there is a reserve price, and either the auctioneer or the seller has received or procured the reserve price, the buyer is permitted to refuse the sale and walk away. The buyer's refusal does not revive the previous bid. The buyer's second option is to accept the item and pay the last good faith bid made before the sale was declared complete.

CONDITIONS OF SALE

Conditions for a sale by auction can be different in each state. The ones listed are commonly accepted in most jurisdictions.

- An auction is a public sale by competitive bidding.
- The auctioneer can refuse any bid without offering a reason.
- The highest bidder is the buyer.
- Every buyer is required to provide his name, address and phone number.
- Once the sale is complete, if the buyer refuses to pay, the auctioneer may resell the item and the buyer may be required to pay any difference in selling price.
- Items are sold "as is, where is" with no guarantee or warranty given or implied.
- Buyer is expected to remove the item on sale day or within the timeframe established and published prior to sale day.
- If the buyer does not comply with all sale conditions, he forfeits any moneys paid.

ACCOUNTING

An auctioneer provides a service. He is selling his knowledge and expertise. He is in business to make a profit for his clients and himself. An important part of any successful business is record keeping. Producing and maintaining accurate records is a must for several reasons. The federal government as well as many state and local governments require records be kept from three (3) to seven (7) years. If an audit is ever requested, some or all of these records will have to be produced for review. The auctioneer should store records where they will not deteriorate and can be accessed easily. In order to avoid problems including fines and penalties, it is important to follow all the pertinent rules and regulations, request and complete any necessary permits, file all required forms and pay any and all fees and taxes in a timely manner.

Auctioneer Responsibilities

The auctioneer's focus should always be on the seller. The auctioneer acts as the seller's agent during the appraisal process, preparing and executing the advertising campaign, while answering questions about the seller's property and during the sale itself. The auctioneer's main goal is to obtain the best selling price for every item entrusted to his care by the client.

The auctioneer also has a responsibility to the buyer. When the auctioneer accepts a bid and closes the sale, the buyer is, in effect, appointing the auctioneer his agent. It is the auctioneer's responsibility to write down the successful buyer's name, the lot number of the item purchased and the price to be paid. If the auctioneer does not record the required information about the sale properly and comply with all the regulations of the locality where the sale is held, the buyer is under no obligation to take possession of or pay for the goods.

Invoices

An invoice, also called a receipt, is a detailed list of all the items purchased by a buyer at the sale. It includes but is not limited to:

- Date of the sale. - Name of the auctioneer and/or auction company.
- Address and phone number of the auction company.
- Buyer's name and billing address. - Bidder number.
- If appropriate, shipping address and method of transport.
- Method of payment:
  - Cash
  - Check – include check number
  - Credit card – include name of company, account number, expiration date.
  - Bank draft/wire transfer – include bank information and document number.
- Lot number(s) of item(s).
- Quantity of each item. - Brief description of item(s).
- Amount owed for each item.
- Sales tax due. - Balance due.
- Some invoices include a space for notes and general information.
- Invoices should have at least two (2) copies: one for the buyer and one for the auctioneer's records.

Record Keeping

If the auctioneer wants to attract new clients, keep current clients coming back and avoid potentially costly and time-consuming problems with federal, state and local governments, it is essential to establish a reputation for honesty in all transactions. One of ways to do this is by keeping accurate records and filing the required paperwork with all governing jurisdictions as well as providing written documentation to the seller and the buyer. Drafting clear Auction Sales Agreements and presenting accurate settlement statements to the seller and providing detailed bills of sale, invoices and clear titles (if appropriate) to the buyer minimizes questions and helps prevent problems and misunderstandings. Avoiding problems with governing bodies and providing easy-to-understand paperwork to the seller and the buyer is a very effective marketing tool. It assures the potential client the auctioneer plays by the rules and doesn't cut corners.

Sales Reports

A sales report is a summary of all sales transactions made within a specified time frame. The data can show the results for the day of the auction or it can summarize monthly, quarterly and annual totals. If this information is computerized, it can provide an easy way to review sales activity and determine how the business is performing. Depending upon the time frame given and information requested, sales reports can indicate the number of sales completed, total dollars collected and split out sales tax owed or the tax amount that has already been paid.

A sales report can also provide a list of clients. Depending upon the information entered into the database, the auctioneer can use this summary for marketing and advertising purposes because names, addresses and phone numbers are in one place and easy to access. Using reports for multiple purposes is a smart business practice that saves time and money.

1099 Mistakes

If an independent contractor receives a 1099 from a client and the data does not agree with the contractor's files, he should immediately contact the client to discuss the discrepancies. The errors should be fixed and a revised copy sent to both the contractor and the Internal Revenue Service (IRS). An independent contractor should never ignore discrepancies and should always keep a record of agreements, conversations and correspondence with the client just in case the IRS does not receive a corrected 1099. Not following up on these issues with the client and failing to keep records could cause a delay in solving any issues with the IRS.

Bills-of-Sale

A bill-of-sale is a legal document that certifies the transfer of ownership from one person, company or entity to another person, company or entity. In some states this document is required to prove ownership of real property such as real estate, motor vehicles, aircraft, boats, livestock and some large equipment. The new owner needs a bill-of-sale to prove ownership in order to transfer titles and deeds into his name or his company's name.

Some government agencies have an approved form that must be used. It is the auctioneer's responsibility to have these forms available during the sale. Since most states and the federal government require a bill-of-sale in order to transfer ownership of property such as real estate, aircraft and motor vehicles, it is the buyer's responsibility to make sure he has a properly executed document before he leaves the sale site. The auctioneer should give the seller a copy of the bill-of-sale and keep a copy for his files.

Unless the property requires a specific, government approved bill-of-sale, a general format may be used. The auctioneer can develop a form and have copies printed or purchase pre-printed forms from an office supply store. Whichever form is used, spaces for the following information are needed:

- Date of the sale.
- Description of the item purchased.
- Depending upon the item:
    - Make, model, year, serial number.
    - Title number.
    - Vehicle identification number (VIN)
    - For a boat, the hull identification (ID) number.
- Name of the buyer or buyers as it will appear on the title.
- The purchase price.
- Sentence stating the seller(s) is legal owner and has authorization to sell the item.
- Sentence swearing all the data shown is true, complete and accurate.
- Seller or sellers printed name, signature and address.

Some states require the bill-of-sale be witnessed by a Notary Public.

W-2's vs. 1099's

Any person who earns wages of any kind is required to pay income taxes to the Internal Revenue Service (IRS) and in some places, state and local income taxes. The individual will complete either a W-2 or a 1099.

For a person who completes a W-2, the employer deducts the appropriate amount of taxes from the employee's paycheck per the information shown on the W-2, i.e. filing status (single, married), number of exemptions, etc. The employer is responsible for making payments for:

- Employee federal and state income taxes and FICA (Social Security and Medicare).
- Employer's portion of FICA plus FUTA (Federal Unemployment Tax) and SUI (State Unemployment Tax).

A person who is paid via a 1099 is required to pay his or her own federal and state income taxes and both the employee and employer portions of FICA. The individual must also address any workers compensation and unemployment tax issues.

Independent Contractors

An independent contractor is a self-employed individual who performs a service for a client The client is required to report earnings of six hundred dollars ($600.00) or more in one year to the Internal Revenue Service (IRS) and provide the independent contractor with a 1099 by January 31st.

An independent contractor works on his own timeframe, uses his own equipment, hires and compensates any additional people required to complete the job and is usually paid on a per job or per piece rate. The contractor and the client may have a contractual agreement that states each party's responsibilities.

When a person is classified as an independent contractor, the client avoids:

- Withholding federal and state income taxes.
- Paying the employer's portion of Social Security and Medicare taxes.
- Paying federal and state unemployment insurance premiums.
- State disability insurance premiums and workers' compensation costs.
- Providing any fringe benefits.
- Liability for negligence or EEOC non-compliance by the contractor.

Escrow Accounts

An escrow account is used to guarantee the funds paid by the buyer will be preserved until the final settlement with the owner. When money is put into an escrow account it means a third party takes possession of the funds until the seller and/or buyer fulfill the specific conditions of the sale within the time frame stated. Most states require the third party to be a federally insured financial institution, i.e. a bank, credit union, etc. Other money cannot be commingled or mixed with the funds in escrow. The money in escrow cannot be used for any purpose until settlement is reached. This includes but is not limited to paying outstanding auction-related expenses such as appraisal fees, advertising, set up charges, catering costs and the auctioneer's commission.

Collections and Financing

The cashier checks the buyer's name against the master registration list to verify he has a valid bidder number. He totals all purchases made by the bidder as noted on the clerking ticket sheets and collects the amount due from the buyer or his agent. Sometimes representatives from financial institutions are on site to arrange financing. Other times financing terms are arranged prior to the sale and the final figures and other particulars are added after the sale. In most states, all monetary and financial transactions are completed the day of the sale unless alternate arrangements are made prior to the day of the sale. The cashier must be aware of these arrangements. Cash, checks, credit cards, bank drafts and wire transfers are accepted at most sales. Accepted methods of payment are usually stated in all advertising media used to promote the auction. Any restrictions or special requirements should also be noted.

Fund Dispersal

Funds are dispersed according to the conditions set forth in the auction sales agreement. This contract states in detail what services are to be performed by the auctioneer and what expenses the seller approves and who is responsible for each activity. Therefore, no funds are dispersed until all legitimate and agreed to expenses are deducted from the gross proceeds of the sale. If funds are being held in escrow, there can be no final payout of moneys until the conditions for the escrow account are fulfilled and the funds from the escrow account are released. Once the settlement statement is prepared by the cashier, reviewed, agreed to and signed by the auctioneer and the seller, the net proceeds as stated on the settlement statement are given to the seller.

Balancing Accounts

The cashier tallies all the clerking ticket sheets and compares this figure to the total of all moneys collected during the sale. This includes cash, checks, credit card receipts, wire transfers, letters of credit, amounts promised in sealed bids and funds deposited in escrow accounts. In order for the auction accounts to balance, the total on the clerking ticket sheets and total of funds collected must agree. If they do not, the cashier needs to match each individual item on every clerking ticket sheet with each item listed on all the invoices generated that day in order to find and correct the error. The cashier must also make sure he has completed copies of all required forms for the auctioneer's files. The date of the auction and the cashier's name or initials should be on all calculator tapes, clerking ticket sheets, financial reports and any other sale-related documentation.

EINs

The EIN, employer identification number, is also called the federal tax ID number. It is a nine (9) digit number the Internal Revenue Service (IRS) assigns to a business. This number identifies a specific business, just like the social security number identifies a specific individual, and tells the IRS this owner is required to file various business tax returns monthly, quarterly and annually. The business owner can obtain an employer identification number online at the Internal Revenue Service web site, www.irs.gov, or by mail or telephone. If the owner lives in a state that participates in the Federal Employer Identification Number project, application can be made at a local IRS office. Before the owner can file any tax returns, the business must have an EIN. Since it may take a few weeks to receive the EIN from the IRS, the application should be made as soon as possible after the business is established.

The IRS requires a business to have an EIN if the business:

- Has employees.
- Is a corporation or a partnership.
- Is required to pay employment, excise, alcohol, tobacco or firearms taxes.
- Withholds taxes on income paid to a non-resident alien.
- Has a Keogh retirement plan.
- Involves trusts, estates, real estate, mortgage investments, non-profit farmers' cooperatives or plan administrators.

If a business owner is unsure whether he needs an EIN, he should consult an accountant for advice.

Settlement Statements

The settlement statement or summary sheet is a detailed accounting of the financial aspects of the sale. The format may vary but the information is standard. The following data is provided:

- Date of the sale. - Name of the auctioneer.
- Name and address of the owner. - Total income from the sale.

Expenses can include but are not limited to:

- Auctioneer's fee.
- Appraisal costs.
- Advertising costs
- Staff salaries
- Catering costs
- Supplies
- Miscellaneous
- Sales tax

With his signature, the auctioneer is certifying the financial accounting is complete and accurate. With his signature, the seller is accepting the financial accounting and agrees to accept the net sale figure.

Unsold Items

If an item does not sell at or above the reserve price or the auctioneer withdraws an item from the sale for any reason, the property is usually returned to the seller. Sometimes the method of return is outlined in the Auction Sales Agreement. If the disposition of unsold items is not addressed in the contract, the auctioneer needs to make arrangements to remove the items from the auction site. Depending upon the reason for the sale, the item may be returned to the seller, may be held by the auction company at another location for a future auction or may be donated to a charity. If the item is being sold because of a lien or government confiscation, the auctioneer needs to comply with the applicable state and/or federal law governing such occurrences.

Releasing Merchandise

It is the auctioneer's responsibility to make sure all the property sold and any related paperwork is completed and released to the correct buyers. Even though most items are sold "as is, where is" with no warranty or guarantee given or implied, the merchandise needs to be inspected before it is released to verify the items are in the same condition as when the buyer bid on them. He also needs be sure items are given to the right buyer and that one buyer's goods are not mixed up with another buyer's goods. Whoever is delegated to perform this function should check the lot number on the invoice, receipt or bill-of-sale with the lot number on the item. He should also make sure the invoice has been marked "paid." Any questions or disputes should be resolved immediately. The cashier may need to be consulted for verification of payment.

Records

The federal government requires certain records be kept for a specific number of years. Many state governments have a similar list and retention requirement. Some local jurisdictions may also have requirements for the length of time specific records must be preserved. It is the auctioneer's responsibility to comply with all government regulations. Ignorance of the law is never accepted as a valid reason for non-compliance.

The federal government requires the following paperwork be retained for tax and audit purposes. Wherever the auctioneer conducts business, he should check with the appropriate state commissions and local agencies for their particular requirements. Required copies include but may not be limited to:

- Master registration sheets. - Contracts with the seller, advertising media, vendors, labor, etc. - Checks sent and received.
- Credit card receipts. - List of cash receipts. - Invoices/receipts.
- Advertising collateral. - Calculator tapes.
- Video, audio and digital tape recordings.
- Any other pertinent documents not listed.

Sales Tax

Sales tax is a levy placed on the retail price of merchandise and, in some states, services sold to the public. The state legislature determines what merchandise is levied and which services pay sales tax. The legislature determines the percentage of the sale price each business must collect, i.e. 8.25%. State sales tax amounts are usually set by the state legislature and enforced by the state comptroller's office. Cities and counties may have sales tax requirements in addition to the state sales tax. These sales taxes are set by the city council and elected county officials. City and county sales tax payments are made to the tax assessor collector's office. Depending upon the amount of money collected, sales tax is paid on a monthly, quarterly or annual basis. The business or person collecting sales tax must apply for and receive a sales tax permit from the state prior to charging and collecting sales tax.

Every jurisdiction has a list of the merchandise and services for which sales tax must be collected. It is the responsibility of the auctioneer, the clerk and the cashier to be familiar with, understand and comply with all sales tax requirements. Sales tax is collected from the buyer at the time payment is made for a taxable item. Every sales tax jurisdiction exempts certain organizations from paying sales tax; for example: churches, charitable groups, non-profit organizations. Qualifying groups must apply for a sales tax exemption certificate. The exemption requirements vary for every taxing authority. Sometimes this exemption is only on certain goods and services; other times it covers anything purchased by the exempt group. If the buyer claims the purchase is tax exempt, he must provide a copy of the sales tax exemption certificate at the time of payment. Most taxing authorities require a copy of the exemption certificate be filed with the tax payment.

Religious, educational and charitable groups and organizations classified by the Internal Revenue Service (IRS) as 501(c) are exempt from sales tax as long as the goods are made by members of the group or are donated to the organization. The donated item cannot be sold to the original donor. The organization and each affiliated chapter are able to conduct two (2) sales a year. Each sale can only be one (1) day long. If a sale runs more than twenty-four (24) consecutive hours, a second sale cannot be held during the same calendar year.

If the group hires an auctioneer, he can be paid a reasonable fee for his services. In some states "reasonable fee" is defined as no more than twenty percent (20%) of the gross proceeds. In most states, if any exemption requirement is violated, the certificate is revoked and the sales tax must be paid. Fines and/or penalties can be assessed.

Sales made by senior citizens' groups are also exempt from sales tax if the items sold are produced, made or assembled exclusively by people sixty-five (65) years or older. The sale must be a fund-raiser sponsored by a non-profit group that assists the elderly. The profits must all be given to the group and the organization cannot hold more than four (4) such sales per year.

University and college student organizations are exempt from sales tax if the group is recognized by an accredited college or university and provides the states comptroller's office with proof of its affiliation with that institution. The university may provide a comprehensive list of organizations to the state so each group does not have to file separately. Each group's primary function cannot be a profit-producing venture. The organization cannot hold more than one (1) sale per calendar month and most states have restrictions on the total dollar amount that can be collected.

Other organizations may be considered exempt from paying sales tax:

- Non-profit Chamber of Commerce devoted to promoting business in the area it represents.
- Non-profit convention and tourist agency recognized by a municipality.
- Electric cooperative as defined by the state in which it operates.
- Telephone cooperative as defined by the state in which it operates.
- Local organizing committee authorized by a city, county or the state to prepare and present a bid to host an international athletic event.

Some states may recognize some or all of these groups while some states may include others and exclude some of these. The auctioneer should be familiar with the groups ordinarily found exempt in the state in which he operates.

A non-profit charitable organization devotes all its activities to addressing the relief of poverty, disease, pain and suffering of indigent and/or low-income people. The group may provide food, clothing, specialized treatment, shelter or counseling with funds supplied by or collected from sources other than the persons served. The organization cannot charge clients fees for any service provided.

A non-profit educational group or government entity engages solely in instruction in the arts, sciences and vocations. The group must have a published curriculum and a faculty of qualified instructors must use common teaching methods. Students must be enrolled and attend classes in an educational environment. Programs offering discussion groups, forums, panels and lectures may also qualify.

A non-profit religious organization is a group of people who meet regularly to conduct worship services according to the tenets of their religion. They must be able to provide proof of an established congregation who attend scheduled meetings.

Most states recognize certain groups as automatically exempt from paying sales tax without the need to apply for and prove their exempt status. The group is required to provide the state comptroller's office with verification of its exempt status. This list includes but is not limited to:

- All executive, legislative and judicial branches of the United States Government including: boards, committees, commissions, agencies, military entities, any corporation wholly (100%) owned by the US Government.
- Federal Credit Unions organized under Article 12 United States Code 1768.
- State, city and county agencies.
- Any college or university created or authorized by the state.
- Any organization whose purpose is to answer fire alarms and extinguish fires or provide emergency medical services whose volunteers receive little or no compensation.
- Non-profit health and agricultural development corporations for items for their use and benefit only. Does not apply to items to be lent, sold, leased or rented.

In order to qualify for automatic exemption from sales tax, most states require organizations meet all the qualifications shown.

- Formed only to conduct exempt activities.
- Operations must be devoted exclusively to exempt activities.
- All assets must be dedicated to exempt activities.
- No shareholder or private individual may profit directly or indirectly from goods or services provided by the organization.
- Salaries and any other benefits paid to offices and employees must reflect actual services performed.

Most states require specific paperwork be submitted to qualify for exempt status. All submitted documentation is reviewed and considered when making the exempt determination. Documents include but may not be limited to:

- Written statement outlining specific activities, services, income, assets and liabilities.
- Copy of the articles of incorporation, if applicable.
- Copy of the bylaws.
- Copy of its trust agreement, if applicable.
- Copy of letter from the Internal Revenue Service granting exemption.

In some states, sales tax must be collected from the client if sales tax was not charged at the time the item was originally purchased. If the auctioneer charges the client more for the goods and/or services than he paid the vendor when he made the purchase, the entire cost is subject to sales tax even if sales tax was paid at the time of the original purchase. The following is a partial list of expenses that may be exempt from sales tax in some states. The auctioneer needs to be familiar with the list of exempt expenses in the areas in which he operates.

- Printing charges by an outside printer.
- Casual labor: runners, set-up crew, etc.
- Replacement or repair parts for items being offered at the sale.
- Advertising and media charges.

Certain auction-related direct expenses may be exempt from sales tax. Specific criteria must usually be met before these expenses can be excluded. Documentation should be available to prove the criteria have been met. The auctioneer needs to be familiar and comply with all applicable statutes and ordinances of the area in which he operates. These are commonly used criteria to determine which direct expense charges may be deducted from the gross proceeds of the sale before the sale tax is computed:

- The purchase is made for a specific client rather than for general use.
- Sales tax is paid when the item is purchased.
- There is no mark-up to the client for the item.
- The item or service is itemized on the client's invoice or receipt.

Note: services or items ordinarily exempt from sales tax may be excluded if the other criteria are met.

In some states, certain expenses may not be charged to the client directly so the client does not pay sales tax on these goods and services. These include but are not limited to:

- W2 salary employees, i.e. people who work directly for the auctioneer or the auction company.
- Services provided in-house such as copying and faxing charges.

- Purchases of equipment and services used in the daily operation of the auctioneer's or the auction company's usual business functions such as computers, general office supplies, legal, accounting and janitorial services, rent for or leasing of office space, telephone and paging services, etc.

It is the auctioneer's responsibility to know about and comply with all applicable state statues and local ordinances in every area in which he operates.

Auction Staff Salaries

Depending upon the particular arrangements an auctioneer has with an auction company, either the auctioneer or the auction company is responsible for paying staff members. Most of the time, if the auctioneer and the staff are employees of the auction company, the company is responsible for paying all personnel. If the auctioneer is an independent businessman who calls auctions for many companies and/or individuals like attorneys disposing of estates and owners who arrange private sales, he is responsible for recruiting, training and paying the necessary staff. Minimum staff needed to conduct most auctions includes a clerk, a cashier and five to seven ring personnel who are usually paid when the auction is over and all related business is completed. Their salaries are one of the expenses shown on the settlement statement. Some auctioneers use the same staff all the time, others recruit as needed.

Resale Certificates

A resale certificate is granted to a person or business that purchases items to be resold to third party. The holder of a resale certificate is required to present a copy of the certificate at the time of payment for merchandise purchased for resale. The cashier acts in good faith when accepting a resale certificate. If any member of the auction staff has reason to believe the buyer does not have a valid resale certificate from the state in which the goods will be resold, the staff member must inform the cashier. It is the auctioneer's responsibility to make sure the correct sales tax is collected or a valid resale certificate is presented. In most states, any person who makes, presents, uses or alters a resale or any other exemption certificate in order to evade paying sales tax is committing a criminal offense and will most likely be prosecuted.

The Uniform Commercial Code

The Uniform Commercial Code is a set of rules and provisions that are written and enacted to simplify and clarify commercial transactions. Most states have a Uniform Commercial Code and while the specifics may be a bit different in each state, there are generally accepted terms and regulations defined and explained in all codes. The code's purpose is to assist the expansion of commercial practices by drafting and enforcing uniform laws that govern all jurisdictions in the state. The standards defined in the code are expected to be applied in good faith with diligence and reason by all the parties involved in a business enterprise. If a transaction involves two (2) or more states or another nation, the provisions of either may be applied as long as all the parties involved agree which code is to be used.

The **seller** has certain rights clearly stated under the Uniform Commercial Code. Individual states may include other rights, but the ones discussed are commonly accepted by most states. If the buyer refuses to take delivery of the item, fails to make the agreed upon payment or payments on the day or days specified in the terms of the sale agreement or the payment is rejected for any reason i.e. insufficient funds, insolvency of the buyer, etc., the seller may:

- Cancel the sale.
- Stop delivery of the item.
- Resell the item to recover any monetary loss incurred.
- Demand return of the title and any other paperwork given to the buyer at the time of the sale.

If the seller cancels the sale and/or stops delivery of the item, he is obligated to notify the buyer within a reasonable amount of time the reason for cancellation and/or stoppage.

The **buyer** has certain rights clearly stated under the Uniform Commercial Code. Individual states may include other rights, but the ones discussed are commonly accepted by most states. When a buyer purchases an item, he receives clear title. He accepts in good faith that the seller legally owned the item and had authorization to sell it and transfer ownership. The buyer has the right to take possession in the time set forth according to the terms of the sale.

The buyer can refuse to take possession of the item if:

- Another party claims ownership.
- The item was damaged or otherwise changed after the sale concluded.
- The seller did not have the authority to sell the item.
- The seller does not turn over the item on the day and at the time agreed.
- The seller does not provide clear title and any other documentation required to transfer ownership.

A **creditor** has certain rights as defined under the Uniform Commercial Code. Individual states may include other rights, but the ones discussed are commonly accepted by most states. If a creditor has a lien against a seller's property or is otherwise owed money, the creditor usually has first claim on the item or the revenue generated when the item is sold to a third party. The creditor can demand the sale be declared null and void if the seller still owes the creditor money and/or if the seller tries to transfer the item to a third party and does not pay the balance due to the creditor. This is one reason why the auctioneer should verify the seller owns the item free and clear before offering the item for sale.

Letters of Credit

A letter of credit (LC) is a guarantee by a financial institution, i.e. a bank, credit union, etc., to honor a legitimate request for payment from a particular account within the amount specified in the document. The applicant is the person requesting the LC; the beneficiary is the person entitled to request payment according to the terms of the LC. A letter of credit is usually very specific about the conditions required before the issuing institution will honor the request. It is always necessary to present the original document before funds will be released. If the LC states payments will be made at specified intervals, arrangements can be made to automatically transfer funds to the beneficiary's account. Both the sending and receiving institutions may have certain procedures to ensure the transfer takes place as required.

To avoid any potential problems, the cashier should verify the terms of the letter of credit before the auction begins.

Bulk Sales Agreements

A bulk sales agreement is a legal contract that specifies what stock or inventory is being transferred, where the items are stored and how long the buyer has to remove the items from their current location. It specifies the earnest money or down payment required before the buyer begins taking inventory and/or is allowed to remove any items from their current location. It further states how the items will be paid for and, if the funds are to be placed in escrow, which federally insured financial institution will hold the funds. The contract outlines what happens if the items are not as described. It also includes any other conditions that must be met by the seller and the buyer. The agreement details how, where and when the transfer of title will take place. The seller and the buyer sign the agreement. Some states require a Notary Public witness the document.

Transfers of Funds

Transferring funds from one financial institution to another, i.e. a bank, credit union, etc. is governed by the banking requirements of the state in which the institution operates. If the institution is located in several states, each branch is subject to the rules and regulations of the state in which it operates.

When funds are transferred between two states, the obligations between the sender and the receiving institution are governed by the regulations of the receiving state. The obligations of the beneficiary and his financial institution are governed by the state in which the beneficiary's institution is located.

In order to simplify the transfer of funds between states with different regulations, in some jurisdictions, the sending and receiving institutions may agree to abide by the procedures of just one state.

In order to avoid potential problems, the auctioneer and cashier should understand and comply with the requirements for the transfer of funds.

Contracts

A contract is a legally binding promise that explains what each party (person) agrees to do, to provide or to act on in exchange for adequate consideration. Adequate consideration is the benefit(s) the person can reasonably expect to receive if he agrees to the contract. A contract may be a written document or a verbal agreement and a handshake. Both versions are recognized and enforced by the states' legal systems and the federal judiciary. Contracts are usually regulated by state statutes, common law (judge-made rulings) and private law. Private law covers the terms of the agreement between the people making the promise(s). In some states, private law may take precedence over state or common law. Contracts should never be entered into unless all parties understand the entire agreement. In order for the contract to be legally binding, all signers must be of legal age (in most states eighteen) and of sound mind (able to understand the terms of the agreement).

Legal Liabilities

In any industry, there are always legal obligations or liabilities. The auction business is no different. That is why it is imperative for the auctioneer and/or the auction company to establish written standards to ensure ethical business practices by the staff. The procedures won't totally eliminate possible problems but they will help minimize costly and time-consuming lawsuits that can result. Part of the company culture should include knowing, understanding and complying with all applicable federal laws, state statutes and local ordinances. It is also a prudent decision to have liability insurance to protect company assets. In some states, the personal assets of owners, board members and shareholders can also be affected in a legal dispute so the auctioneer should consider business liability insurance for himself as well.

Contract Law Responsibilities

Even though an auctioneer is not usually a licensed attorney therefore cannot practice law, he needs to be aware of and comply with all the rules and regulations governing contracts in the state or states in which he operates. He needs to be able to read and understand the legal language used in most contracts. The Sales Auction Agreement is a contract that binds the client and the auctioneer to specific provisions concerning the auction. The Bill of Sale is a contract that promises the buyer certain conditions have been or will be met. The auctioneer may use pre-printed documents but blank spaces still need to be filled in correctly. It is important to be familiar with the statutes so the auctioneer does not make mistakes while drafting contracts. His knowledge protects himself, his staff and the auction company from potentially costly and time-consuming litigation.

Legal Obligations

The seller should be authorized to offer the item for sale and provide clear title and any other documentation (if applicable) required to transfer ownership. He should be willing to verify authenticity of the item or have an expert examine it. He should deliver the item to the sale site by the agreed time or arrange transport. He should be of legal age to enter into a binding contract with the auctioneer and to sign a bill of sale.

The buyer should be of legal age to purchase the item. He should be old enough to legally sign and accept a properly executed bill of sale. He should pay promptly with cash, check, credit card, wire transfer or letter of credit and, if applicable, agree to have the funds placed in escrow. He should collect the purchased item(s) at the appointed time and make arrangements to remove the item from the sale location as required.

The auctioneer should make a good faith effort to verify ownership and authenticity of the property and the client's authorization to sell the item. Contracts need to be properly worded, signed and witnessed according to applicable laws. Advertising must be accurate and truthful. If an enterprise is not going out of business, it should not be advertised that it is. The auction site needs to be set up appropriately for the type of sale being held. Examples: aisles should be kept clear of trash and debris; motor vehicle auction sites should have signs posted directing foot traffic and indicating vehicle roadways. All money handling procedures and record keeping functions must conform to standard accounting practices and meet Internal Revenue Service regulations. Everything should be done to encourage safety procedures to prevent accidents to people and property. This is a small sample of the auctioneer's responsibilities regarding legal liabilities.

Vehicle Titles

In most states, title to motor vehicles, including trailers, must be transferred within thirty (30) days of purchase. There are certain motor vehicles exempt from this requirement. These vehicles may vary from state to state but the ones listed are commonly included. Vehicles that are:

- Owned by the United States government.
- Owned by a manufacturer or dealer and being held for sale.
- Owned by a non-resident but with a current title issued by his state of residence.
- Engaged in interstate transportation of people and/or goods with a current title issued by another state or country.
- Moved solely by animal power.
- Self-propelled wheelchairs and invalid tricycles.
- Trailers with a gross weight of less than three thousand (3000) pounds.
- Manufactured mobile homes as defined by the individual state.

The auctioneer should be familiar with the exemptions in the states in which he operates.

Most states require specific paperwork to transfer the title of a motor vehicle. The seller must surrender the title to the buyer along with an odometer statement. The odometer statement certifies the actual mileage reading on the vehicle's odometer at the time of the sale. Some states also require a bill of sale and a completed vehicle sales tax form.

If the original title was lost, stolen or mutilated, a duplicate title can be obtained from the state's motor vehicle division by completing a form and paying a fee.

Depending upon the state, sometimes this can be accomplished in one day by applying at DMV office in person.

If the odometer reading was stated incorrectly or not noted on the day of the sale, most states require a affidavit attesting to the accurate mileage on the day of the sale. This statement must be signed in the presence of a Notary Public.

Real Estate Titles

A title search is information obtained about the history and current status of real property. This search is conducted primarily to ascertain and verify ownership of real estate and motor vehicles. Other real property usually does not require a title and/or deed. The completed title search may contain but is not limited to copies of all transfers, liens, judgments and any other data recorded about the property at the city or county court house. These documents comprise what is commonly known as a title search.

A title search may be necessary if there is a question about who owns the property and if that person has the right and authority to sell the property and transfer ownership. In the case of real estate, the original plat (detailed drawing and description of the property) and/or the deed may have been lost, stolen or mutilated. In most states, these documents are required to transfer ownership.

A title search on real estate is typically conducted before the completion of the sale. It will discover outstanding contractor liens or judgments and the status of any mortgages on the property. Knowing this financial information can influence the selling price a great deal. This knowledge is important to investors who may plan to purchase the property at a foreclosure proceeding such as an auction and to real estate agents offering a property to a prospective buyer. Some title searches may include comparable sales data on similar property in the area, which can also influence the sale price. A title search may be necessary when a family event occurs such as a divorce or the owner dies without a will and the estate must be probated. A title search helps protect the investor, real estate agent, auctioneer and buyer from unexpected claims against the property before, during and after the sale.

Anyone can conduct a title search because these records are in the public domain i.e. available to the any person. Some states and counties may have other requirements but the ones discussed are commonly used in most states.

To request a motor vehicle title, the vehicle identification number (VIN) and the make, model and year are needed. A search can be done using the title number. To request a title/deed search on real estate, the researcher must know the physical address and name of the owner. If both are unknown, a search for the street or rural route on parcel maps available at the County Assessor's Office will locate the property. Once the address is known, request the assessor's parcel number (APN). With the APN, the County Assessor's Office will issue a current title. With the title number it is possible to obtain past deeds, survey plats and other pertinent data.

Real Estate Sales Requirements

Real estate auctions are growing in popularity and often attract national and international buyers. Auctions are an effective method to sell residential and commercial properties and undeveloped land because they help establish fair prices in a sometimes volatile market. These sales offer organizations (i.e. corporations and fiduciary groups holding real estate assets) an efficient way to sell surplus and/or non-productive properties.

Currently there is a lively debate about what licensing, beyond an auctioneer's license, should be required to sell real estate at auction. Some states require a licensed real estate agent or broker be present at the sale. The National Association of Realtors (NAR) modified its rules to clarify realtors' roles in conducting and participating in real estate auctions. Twenty-four (24) states have passed statues that address this issue. Since each state takes a unique approach and includes different rules, auctioneers must be familiar with the regulations in the states in which they operate.

Trust Accounts

A trust account is a legal and financial agreement to hold, manage and be accountable for someone else's money. Funds are deposited in a financial institution, which is defined as a state or federally chartered bank, credit union, savings and loan association and building and loan association. In order to accept, hold and manage trust accounts, these organizations must be insured by the Federal Deposit Insurance Corporation (FDIC).

Properly payable means the instrument or form presented for payment in a normal course of business must be honored as outlined in the terms of the trust account.

A **notice of dishonor** is the written explanation the financial institution is required by law to give the requester if the financial institution is refusing for any reason to honor the request for payment.

All **interest** earned on the money in a trust account is owed and payable to the client after any services charges and fees required by the financial institution and any taxes owed to the federal, state and local government taxing authorities are deducted. If the trust account will only be active for a short period of time, the trustee may elect to defer payment of any charges, fees or taxes until the funds in the account are disbursed. Any interest earned is automatically deposited into the trust account and is not available to the client, the trustee or anyone else until the funds are distributed. Disbursal of the principle and interest is subject to the time period required by the banking laws of state in which the financial institution operates. Sometimes individual financial institutions will have additional rules on disbursement of funds.

It is a good business practice to maintain accurate records of any funds placed in a trust account. The financial institution is required by law to do so but the auctioneer should also keep a record for his files to answer questions that may arise from the seller or the buyer and help prevent false claims of improper use or disbursal of the funds. The data can be kept like a checkbook register. The minimum information that should be shown includes:

- Date funds received and trust account established (may be different).
- Name and contact information of seller and buyer.
- Lot number and brief description of item(s) involved in the transaction.
- Sale price of the item(s).
- Exact amount of the initial deposit.
- Deposit slip attached.
- Running balance as funds are disbursed to creditors.
- Copies of invoices paid from funds in account attached.
- Notes concerning any transactions made.

Fiduciary is a legal and accounting term that relates to the act of holding money in trust for someone. Specific accounting regulations govern how the funds must be managed and disbursed. Compliance with these rules rests with the financial institution holding the trust account and were established to protect the client, the trustee and the financial institution. Responsibilities include keeping the money in a safe place, maintaining an accurate record of the funds and any interest earned and, when appropriate, disbursal of the funds as mandated by law. Conscientiously following all the rules and regulations offers protection against the possibly of false accusations of financial improprieties with the entrusted funds.

Reports to the client are usually made on a monthly basis. Information should include the current balance in the trust account along with specifics about any dispersal made since the last report. The transaction summary should include the date of payments, name of the creditors, the goods or services received, the amount paid and a copy of the invoices, if available, made since the previous statement.

Record retention varies but is usually three (3) to seven (7) years. The auctioneer should keep a copy of the bill of sale and any other written agreements, the deposit slip from the initial deposit to the account and all subsequent transactions, copies of all invoices, copies of statements sent to the client and any other paperwork associated with the sale.

Most states can order a random audit, or detailed accounting, of trust accounts and will require, at the minimum, the documentation discussed in the previous paragraphs.

Disbursal of the funds placed in a trust account is usually outlined in the bill of sale. It is part of the sale agreement between the seller and the buyer. These terms are included when the account is opened at the financial institution. The mechanics of disbursal are determined by the banking laws of the state in which the holding institution is located. The auctioneer should be familiar with the process in the states in which he operates.

In most states, the only funds available immediately after deposit are cash and wire transfers. Any other form of legal tender must clear the banking system before it becomes collected funds. The number of days required to clear the banking system may vary. The financial institution will provide the date the funds will be available for dispersal. Disbursement of funds can never exceed the balance in the trust account.

Consumer Credit Protection Act

It is against the Consumer Credit Protection Act for any creditor including credit card companies, banks, credit unions and private lending institutions as well as credit reporting agencies to discriminate against any applicant in any part of the credit transaction. The fines and penalties vary depending upon the specific violation.

According to the law, a person cannot be denied credit or discriminated against in any part of a credit transaction based on his or her race, color, religion, national origin, sex, marital status or age (as long as the person is legally old enough to enter into a binding contract).

A person cannot be discriminated against if some or all of his or her income comes from any kind of public assistance program. An applicant cannot be denied credit because he or she insisted upon claiming his or her rights under this law.

Under the Consumer Credit Protection Act and in accordance with the regulations of the Board, it is not considered discrimination to:

- Ask about a person's marital status when the creditor is trying to determine his rights and remedies as applicable to a particular approval of credit.
- Verify the applicant's age in order to determine if he or she is of legal age to enter into a binding contract.
- Ask an elderly person his or her age as long as the elderly person is not given a positive or negative value in any empirically derived credit rating system.
- Request if any of an applicant's income is provided by a public assistance program as long as the inquiry is made in order to determine the person's income level, the probability the income will continue and to learn about his or her credit history.

Credit

Purchasing items on credit enables the borrower to take possession of the item at the time of purchase by agreeing to make payments over a specific period of time. Common forms of financing include credit cards issued by a financial institution and personal loans and mortgages offered by banks, credit unions and other lending institutions. Some merchants offer their own credit options.

Consumer credit is regulated primarily by federal and state laws. Several states have adopted the Uniform Consumer Credit Code to protect consumers and provide guidelines for the credit industry.

The United States Congress passed the Consumer Credit Protection Act to regulate the industry. Provisions include: full disclosure of credit terms; protection from loan sharks; restrictions concerning garnishment of wages; establishment of the National Commission on Consumer Finance which monitors the credit industry including credit card companies and credit reporting agencies.

ZONING

Zoning is the method in which the state, county and local government controls the development of land. Zoning laws specify how land in a particular area may be used, what types of structures are permitted and if and what species of livestock are allowed. Zoning restrictions can also stipulate lot size, the building height and the number of floors allowed and regulate the density of development, which will have a direct impact on the area's population. Some zoning ordinances define and regulate the extraction of any and all natural resources within an area, i.e. water, coal, oil, minerals, etc. Zoning laws will usually provide space for hospitals, public schools, parks, libraries, open spaces and offer protection to historic buildings and other significant community sites.

A **zoning variance** is a request from an individual or business to deviate from all or part of zoning requirement or restriction. It is not a change in the affected ordinance but a waiver of a certain requirement or restriction. There is usually a process to apply for permission to use the land in a way that is ordinarily not permitted in the area. Depending upon the jurisdiction, a hearing before the appropriate board or agency, obtaining a permit and/or paying a fee may be required.

Circumstances that might prompt a request for a variance include but are certainly not limited to:

- Building a gazebo in the back yard of a private home or in a public area.
- Adding a second story to a house or an additional level to a commercial building.
- Altering the placement of a structure on an odd-shaped lot.

Zoning **classifications** are not defined the same in all fifty states and may not be uniform in all jurisdictions of the same state, county or city. Zoning restrictions may not be applied the same way in all communities of the same area either. For example, a combination of residential and commercial may be permitted in one section of a city but not in another area.

Although classifications are not the same in all jurisdictions, the most frequently used ones are:

- Residential may include single-family homes, townhouses and condominiums, apartment communities, hotels, motels, boardinghouses and institutional housing.
- Commercial can be designated for small stores, shopping centers, restaurants, gas stations, entertainment venues and warehouses.
- Industrial can be defined as heavy or light industry and/or research facilities.
- Agricultural includes family-owned farms, farmers' markets and agribusinesses.

"Right of Way"

A "right of way" is an easement granted by the owner of the property that allows the public to travel over the owner's land. This permission should not interfere or be inconsistent with the owner's use of his land or violate any current zoning ordinance. Rights of way started in traditional common law, which defined the rules for access to free flowing water as well as allowing people access to another person's property. Permission to cross private property eventually developed into an informal road system for the local population. Ownership rights are somewhat diminished by granting public access to private property, however, the entire community benefits from the removal of any obstructions to universal freedom of movement.

Public Livestock Auction Market

A public livestock auction market (LAM) is a permanent facility that sells livestock (horses, cattle, goats, sheep, mules, poultry) to the public on a regularly scheduled day or days every week. In most states, a permit is required and must be obtained from the State Veterinarian Board or some other agency as stipulated by the individual state statutes. The permit must be posted for public inspection in a prominent place at the auction site. A person or company operating a livestock auction without a current state issued permit is guilty of a crime, usually a misdemeanor, which is punishable in most states with fines and possible incarceration depending upon the particular situation and/or violations that may be discovered.

It is necessary to maintain the livestock auction site according to specific standards established by the State Veterinary Board. These standards are enforced to prevent the spread of infectious diseases and to provide a clean, and as far as possible, sanitary environment for the animals. The board may inspect required maintenance records at any time. Common standards recognized and required by most states:

- Yards, pens, chutes and areas livestock come in contact with are to be cleaned and disinfected in the approved manner after every sale.
- Areas must be cleaned, raked and sprayed with an approved disinfectant, at least forty-eight (48) hours prior to a sale. Manure and other refuse must be disposed of properly.
- Continuous clean water must be available at all times.
- Adequate feed must be available for animals held overnight.
- Bedding, or the type bedding used, is optional.

In most states in order to obtain a **permit** to operate a public livestock auction market, a person or company must apply to the appropriate state agency, usually the State Veterinarian Board. Requirements include but may not be limited to:

- Petitioner must provide a copy of detailed plans and specifications for the site.
- The state board conducts an inspection of the premises. The petitioner must correct any problems or obtain a waiver for any discrepancies discovered.
- Some specific areas that will be inspected by the board include:
    - The number of pens to hold each species.
    - Separate pens to quarantine possibly infected livestock.
    - Verification of federally mandated square footage for each species.
    - Specific areas to restrain animals for examining, testing and immunizing.
    - Adequate facilities provided for veterinary services.
    - Proper drainage of the entire site.

Most states require a **veterinarian** be present at all public livestock auctions. No sale may be conducted without a representative from the state board present unless the board waives the requirement. The reason for this requirement is to help control and prevent the spread of contagious and infectious diseases. The state board will provide a Doctor of Veterinarian Medicine (DVM).

The veterinarian inspects the auction site to verify all regulations have been met and that the pens, chutes and holding areas are clean and properly maintained. He may review existing documentation for all the animals being offered for sale that day. The veterinarian, or an assistant under his direction, will examine each animal, conduct the required tests and perform any necessary and appropriate treatment(s). If needed, he will quarantine any infected or possibly infected animals. The livestock auction operator is expected to render any help or assistance as requested by the veterinarian.

The state board requires certain **records** be kept by the operator of a public livestock auction market on every animal that passes through the facility. These records may vary from state to state but the ones discussed are commonly required by most states. These records must be retained for two (2) to five (5) years depending upon the individual state. The state board may request to review these records as long as reasonable notice is given to the livestock market operator.

- The name, address and picture identification (i.e. driver's license) of the seller and the buyer.
- Proof of all tests taken and the results of each one.
- Certificates of veterinary inspections and any other required permits and health certificates.
- The unique identifier used as the federally required identification, i.e. ear tags, ear notches, tattoos, brands, etc.
- Purebred papers and any other pertinent registration certification.

Miscellaneous Information About Public Livestock Auction Markets

The auction operator is required to properly identify all livestock with the appropriate ear tag, bangle tag, slap tattoo or backtag as the animal is received at the auction site and at all times while on the animal is on premises.

The permit holder and any person associated with him is required to comply with all applicable laws and regulations. They are expected to cooperate with the State Veterinarian Board and its authorized agents. Penalties, fines, revocation of the permit and, depending upon the seriousness of the offence, prison time may result for failure to comply.

Failure to keep maintenance records for the property and required documentation on all the animals can also result in fines, penalties and possible prison time.

In most states, people who only trade or sell livestock they have raised for themselves or under contract to another entity or animals they have had in their possession for at least sixty (60) days are exempt from these regulations.

Bureau of Alcohol, Tobacco, Firearms and Explosives

The Bureau of Alcohol, Tobacco, Firearms and Explosives, commonly known as the ATF, is an agency of the federal government and part of the US Department of the Treasury. The agency grew out of activities during the Prohibition era of the 1920s. Current ATF agents are the descendants of the legendary Eliot Ness and the revenue agents known as the Untouchables.

Today the agency's mission is to help to prevent terrorism and reduce violent crime by enforcing federal laws and regulating the firearms and explosives industries. They work independently and in partnership with state agencies to investigate crimes involving firearms, explosives, arson and the illegal trafficking of alcohol and tobacco. They are responsible for controlling the production, labeling and advertising of alcohol and tobacco products. They govern the relationship between producers, wholesalers and retailers and protect consumers from impure, mislabeled or harmful products.

Most states have detailed codes that address issues relating to the labeling, shipment, storage and sale of alcoholic beverages, the minimum age required to purchase and consume alcohol in public places and penalties for drunk driving. Private groups like MADD (Mothers Against Drunk Driving) continue to lobby state legislatures to pass tougher restrictions about the consumption of alcohol and harsher penalties for alcohol-related actions especially those acts that cause injury. States have stiff fines and penalties for violating their liquor laws. Most require a license to sell any type of alcoholic beverage. The licensing requirements vary from state to state but most have very strict rules and restrictions as to who will and will not be granted a license to produce, transport and sell alcohol. In some states, local jurisdictions, i.e. cities and counties, also have the authority to deny the production and/or sale of alcoholic beverages within their borders.

The states regulate tobacco use by their citizens. The states determine the age at which people may purchase tobacco products; the penalties for selling tobacco products to minors; the location of stores, vending machines and other methods of distribution; the placement of advertising in proximity to places where minors congregate; the penalties to minors who purchase or attempt to purchase tobacco products. Retailers are required to obtain a permit to sell tobacco products. They must educate their employees and post signs explaining the regulations concerning the sale of tobacco. In some states, after eight (8) offenses in a two-year period, the retailer's permit can be suspended or revoked. A violation by a minor can result in a fine, community service and/or suspension of his driver's license.

States that grow tobacco have specific laws regulating the tobacco industry. It is the auctioneer's responsibility to understand and comply with all the rules, regulations and procedures concerning the growth, production and sale of tobacco products in these states.

The ATF (Bureau of Alcohol, Tobacco, Forearms and Explosives) is responsible for enforcing and ensuring compliance with the following laws enacted by the United States Congress:

- Federal Alcohol Administration Act of 1935.
- Internal Revenue Code (IRS) concerning distilled spirits, tobacco products and firearms.
- Gun Control Act of 1968.
- Title XI of the Organized Crime Control Act, i.e. Explosives Control Act of 1970.
- Parts of the Arms Export Control Act of 1976.
- Trafficking in Contraband Cigarettes Act of 1978.
- Anti-Arson Act of 1982.
- Armed Career Criminal Act of 1984.

Hazardous Waste

Hazardous waste contains properties that are dangerous or potentially harmful to humans and/or the environment, i.e. air, water, ground. Hazardous waste can be liquid, solid, gas and sludge. They can be by-products of a manufacturing process or specific products like cleaning fluids, solvents, chemicals and pesticides. The Environmental Protection Agency (EPA) has determined that specific wastes are always hazardous and has categorized these substances into the following lists:

- F-list contains non-specific source wastes from manufacturing and industrial processes. Since they can occur in various parts of the process, they are called non-specific wastes.
- K-list contains source-specific wastes that are produced by specific industries like petroleum refining and pesticide manufacturing.
- P-list and U-list contain discarded commercial chemical products. Some pesticides, drugs and drug-related products are shown on these two lists.

According to the Environmental Protection Agency (EPA), treatment of hazardous waste is any process that changes the physical, chemical or biological character of waste to make it less of an environmental threat*. The treatment can neutralize the substance, recover energy or natural resources, make the substance less toxic or prepare the waste for transport, storage or disposal. A common treatment method is incineration, which destroys the dangerous components in the substance and reduces the amount of waste. Sometimes the resulting ash may need treatment before it can be put into a landfill. The EPA has developed strict standards for approved treatment of hazardous waste. These options are defined in the Technology Codes and Description of Technology-Based Standards.

According to the Environmental Protection Agency (EPA), waste that does not appear on one of their hazardous waste lists (F, K, P, U), can be classified hazardous if it exhibits one of four characteristics.

- Ignitable waste starts fires under certain conditions, spontaneously combusts or has a low flash point. Waste oils and used solvents are two examples. Several tests can determine if a substance is ignitable.
- Corrosive waste is capable of corroding metal such as storage tanks, drums and barrels. Battery acid is one example.
- Reactive waste is unstable. It can cause explosions, toxic fumes, gases and vapors when heated, compressed or mixed with water. Lithium-sulfur batteries are one example.
- Toxic waste is harmful and/or fatal when swallowed or absorbed through the skin. Mercury and lead are examples. Toxic waste can contaminate the ground and leach into water sources.

According to the Environmental Protection Agency (EPA), hazardous waste must be **disposed of** in facilities that are designed and maintained to contain the hazardous material and prevent any potentially harmful substances from contaminating the air, water or ground. The waste must be treated according to strict EPA standards before it is placed into a permanent storage facility. Solid hazardous waste is usually put in appropriate devices and placed in a landfill, surface impoundment or waste pile. Liquid hazardous waste is usually disposed of in an underground injection well. Because of the potential impact on surface and ground water sources, these wells are regulated under the Safe Drinking Water Act and by the Underground Injection Control Program.

Storing hazardous waste means holding the substance for a short time before it is treated, disposed of or moved. Storage facilities are defined in the Resource Conservation and Recovery Act (RCRA).

- Containers are portable devises use to store, transport, treat or dispose of hazardous waste. They include 55-gallon drums, tanker trucks, railroad cars, buckets and test tubes.
- Tanks are open-topped or enclosed containers made of steel, plastic, fiberglass or concrete.
- Drip pads are wood-drying structures made of non-earthen material.
- Containment buildings are enclosed structures with four walls, a roof and a floor.
- Waste piles are open areas over a double liner system designed so waste does not contaminate land or water sources.
- Surface impoundments are natural depressions, man-made excavations, a holding pond or storage pit. They are lined with plastic to prevent leaching.

An underground storage tank system (UST) can be one or a combination of several tanks. Any pipes connected to the system that have at least ten percent (10%) of their volume underground are part of the UST. The entire tank system is comprised of the tank(s), all underground piping connected to the tanks, ancillary equipment buried underground and any connected containment system. The federal government regulates underground storage tank systems that store petroleum products or specific hazardous substances. Some states and local governments may have additional requirements for underground storage tanks.

Some underground storage tank systems only need to meet federal regulations if used to clean up and/or contain a release of certain substances. Examples include:

- Tanks constructed in the field.
- Systems storing radioactive materials.
- Systems that are part of emergency generator systems at a nuclear power facility.
- Fuel distribution systems at airports.

The owner or operator of a federally regulated underground storage tank system (UST) is required to meet certain standards. Some states have additional regulations. It is the responsibility of the owner or operator to understand and comply with all applicable federal, state and local laws, rules and procedures.

The owners of federally regulated underground storage tank systems must:

- Register with the applicable regulatory agency, board or commission.
- Meet leak detection requirements.
- Meet approved financial responsibilities.
- Perform an approved inspection of the site and take correction action when there is a spill, leak or overflow.
- Follow all rules and procedures when installing new tanks and closing used tanks.
- Maintain required records.
- Periodically inspect corrosion protection and leak detection systems.

The owner or operator of an underground storage tank system (UST) has certain reporting responsibilities. He should be familiar with the requirements of the regulatory agency in the area in which the UST is located. Some have additional or stricter requirements than the ones discussed below, however, these are commonly required by all federal, state and local UST regulatory agencies. A report must be made to the appropriate regulatory agency when:

- A new underground storage tank system is installed. A notification form must be completed which provides specific information about the UST and includes certification the UST has been installed properly.
- A release of the stored substance is suspected. If confirmed, the plan and/or specific actions taken to correct any damage caused by the release.
- Planning to permanently close the UST, a written notification is required thirty (30) days prior to actual shut down.

Specific records are required and must be available for inspection by a representative of the agency that regulates the particular UST. The record retention time varies depending upon the agency, the records in question and the area in which the UST is located. If the owner/operator is in doubt, the records should be kept. Records with the following information should be retained and available for inspection:

- Leak detection performance and maintenance
    - Previous year's monitoring results plus the most recent test results.
    - Manufacturer's performance claims.
    - Maintenance, repair and calibration of on-site detection equipment.
- Inspections and tests of the corrosion protection equipment.
- Any repairs and/or upgrades per approved specifications.
- After permanent closure, site assessment results showing the impact on the surrounding area.
- Complete and accurate documentation concerning financial responsibilities.

Besides the standard requirements for underground storage tank systems (UST), hazardous material USTs must have secondary containment and interstitial monitoring. Enclosing the primary tank with a second wall and monitoring the space between the two walls contains leaks and detects problems before the hazardous substance can harm the environment.

Descriptions of secondary containment:

- Putting one tank or pipe inside another tank or pipe to create a double wall system.
- Putting the UST inside a concrete vault.
- Lining the area with a material that cannot be penetrated by the hazardous material.

Monitoring the space between the two walls is called interstitial monitoring. Regulations describing approved methods and acceptable devices are available from the regulatory agencies.

A variance to these regulations can be obtained by submitting a written request that includes detailed studies of the affected site, the proposed leak detection method and plans for corrective actions.

If there is a confirmed or suspected **release** of a hazardous substance into the environment, several actions are mandated by the regulatory agency and must be taken by the owner or operator of an underground storage tank system (UST).

- To protect the health and safety of people close to the site, immediately take appropriate steps to stop the release and contain what has already been released.
- Report spills or overfills of the hazardous substance to the National Response Center immediately and the regulatory agency involved within twenty-four (24) hours.
- Depending upon the decisions of the agency, a corrective action plan describing in detail how the release will be contained and cleaned up may be required. The approved actions must be implemented as soon as possible and should always be documented.

Water Conservation Activities

The Environmental Protection Agency (EPA) is involved with various activities and works with other federal and state agencies, private industry and environmental organizations to develop plans to protect the environment and manage water resources and the adjacent land using a watershed protection approach. The EPA encourages integrated activities by:

- Developing guidelines to link wetlands protection with watershed planning.
- Providing funding to the states for watershed projects.
- Integrating watershed projects into the federal floodplain plans.
- Supporting national and regional meetings to discuss wetlands and watershed planning programs.

The EPA issues periodic reports on the condition of the nation's wetlands, watersheds and floodplains. One of the agency's missions is to preserve, protect and maintain the quality of our water resources. They are accountable to the American people for the success or failure of their efforts.

Wetlands are a link between land and water resources. Programs to protect wetlands usually work with programs designed to protect and manage other surface and ground water systems. These programs include storm, flood and pollution control, protection of fish and wildlife and creation and maintenance of public recreation areas.

A **watershed** or drainage basin is the area where water, sediment and other material flows from land into a body of water, i.e. river, lake, ocean, and sea. Watershed conservation programs take a systemic approach and consider the entire ecosystem including water, air and land.

A **floodplain** is a low area of land next to a body of water. Floodplains and adjacent water resources form a complex, dynamic ecosystem, which provides flood and erosion control, water filtering, natural habitats for plants and animals and areas for public recreation and scientific study.

Occupational Safety and Health Administration

The Occupational Safety and Health Administration (OSHA) is an agency of the federal government and part of the US Department of Labor. The agency is charged with protecting the health and safety of working men and women throughout America. OSHA works in partnership with employers and employees through inspections, education, training and outreach programs. Besides investigators who review complaints, the agency employs engineers, physicians, educators, writers and technical and support people.

Inspecting the workplace environment is a primary responsibility of OSHA. Because of strong, effective enforcement over the last thirty (30) years, job-related injuries and illnesses have declined by forty-two percent (42%) while employment has more than doubled. One of the reasons for this improvement is many employers voluntarily upgrade working conditions. Companies schedule mandatory safety meetings, create internal safety committees and publicly recognize and reward individuals and departments who continually exhibit safe work place practices.

Review Video: Intro to OSHA
Visit mometrix.com/academy and enter code: 913559

US Army Corp of Engineers

The US Army Corps of Engineers is a decentralized organization that is responsible for protecting navigation on the nation's waterways. The corps tries to keep controls, permits and required paperwork to a minimum. They believe an applicant requesting a permit should receive a quick response. They are responsible for specific activities in US waters including:

- Dams and dikes.
- Excavation, dredging and disposal activities.
- Construction of artificial islands and installations on the continental shelf.
- Dumping of dredged material into US waterways.
- Transporting dredged material for disposal in the oceans.
- Issuing permits for some waterway-related activities.

Reducing Injuries

One of the main things an employer can do to reduce accidents and injuries in the workplace is to promptly and thoroughly investigate all incidents including ones that almost happen. Looking into these occurrences discovers underlying issues. Immediately taking appropriate corrective action helps prevent future accidents and injuries. Having a safety program with written safety rules that are known and understood by all employees is another vital tool. A management team that addresses even minor infractions and applies the rules fairly while recognizing and rewarding safe work place practices clearly demonstrates to employees that the company takes safety issues very seriously.

OSHA (The Occupational Safety and Health Administration) has brochures, posters and training materials available to educate both the employee and the employer. Trade associations, insurance companies and private consultants may also help establish and maintain safety programs.

Job-Related Injury Requirements

The Occupational Safety and Health Administration (OSHA) has specific requirements for covered employers. If a worker is killed, three or more workers are hospitalized or someone has a fatal heart attack, the employer must report the incident to OSHA within eight (8) hours. Employers who do not have easy access to a medical facility must be equipped to provide first aid. Along with adequate first aid supplies, someone is required to be trained and readily available to provide appropriate assistance. Employers are encouraged to have an automated external defibrillator (AED) on site. This device can revive someone having a heart attack. These machines are lightweight, safe and easy to use. Having an automated external defibrillator available can improve the person's chance of survival.

If a serious accident or injury occurs, it is everyone's responsibility to not panic, remain calm and quickly follow the instructions of emergency personnel.

Record Requirements

Employers in industries covered by OSHA (the Occupational Safety and Health Administration) are required to keep a detailed log at each company location of all job-related accidents, injuries and illnesses. This record shows the date and exact location, name of the person(s) involved, a detailed description of the incident and an explanation of the steps taken to address the situation. Every year a summary of these incidents must be posted in a prominent place accessible by all employees and be displayed from February 1st through April 30th.

If an employee is absent from work because of an accident, illness or injury, he is required to present a doctor's return to work permit. This medical release should clearly explain if the doctor has ordered any restrictions on the employee's activities. The employer must respond accordingly. Illnesses and injuries reported to OSHA are not necessarily covered by Workman's Compensation Insurance.

Restricted Duty

The Occupational Safety and Health Administration (OSHA) requires a medical doctor's release before an employer allows an employee to return to work. Depending upon the nature of the injury or illness, the doctor may permit the employee to come back to work only if he or she is assigned restricted duty, also called light duty. This means the employer needs to determine if the person's job responsibilities can be modified to accommodate whatever restrictions the doctor has prescribed. As an alternative, the employer may assign other duties appropriate to the employee's capabilities. If due to the nature of the job, neither of these options is possible, the employee cannot return to work until he or she is able to perform his or her job functions just as he or she could before the illness or injury occurred.

The Occupational Safety and Health Administration (OSHA) has issued guidelines to help an employer determine if an incident should be recorded on the accident, injury and illness log. It is not necessary to record the incident if it only required minor first aid such as:

- Non-prescription medications.
- Cleaning or soaking skin wounds.
- Covering wounds with plain/elastic bandages, gauze pads, wraps, back belts, eye patches, etc.
- Using hot, cold or massage therapy.
- Relieving fingernail or toenail pressure or draining blisters.
- Using a cotton swab or irrigating the eye to remove a foreign object.
- Using tweezers, a cotton swab or other such devices to remove a foreign object from the body.
- Offering fluids to relieve heat-related symptoms.

OSHA Reporting Log

OSHA (The Occupational Safety and Health Administration) has guidelines explaining when an employer should omit the employee's name and write in "privacy case" on the reporting log. When the illness or injury:

- Involves an intimate body part or reproductive system.
- Results from a sexual assault.
- Is a mental illness, HIV, hepatitis or tuberculosis.

- Caused by an object contaminated with a potentially infectious substance.
- If the employee requests his or her name not be shown on the log.

If the employee's name is not entered on the OSHA log, the employer must keep a separate, confidential file with all pertinent information. If the data needed to provide a detailed description of the incident, injury or illness might provide enough information to violate the employee's privacy, the employer may use discretion describing the incident, injury or illness.

Auctioneer Practice Test

1. What is the general rule regarding collecting sales taxes on items sold at an auction?

a. The auctioneer turns over sales receipts to the county taxing authority, which bills buyers.
b. Items sold at auction are generally not subject to sales taxes.
c. The seller should collect sales taxes from buyers on the day of the auction.
d. The auctioneer should collect sales taxes from buyers on the day of the auction.

2. What is the purpose of using an escrow service?

a. It allows the auctioneer to use online payment processors.
b. It protects the buyer from fraud.
c. It protects the seller from fraud.
d. It protects both the buyer and the seller from fraud.

3. An auctioneer is calling bids for an antique dresser. Bidding started at $100. It is up to $350 when the seller suddenly informs the auctioneer he has changed his mind about selling the item. He wants the auctioneer to withdraw the item from the auction. Should the auctioneer withdraw it, or should he or she complete the bidding process and sell it to the highest bidder?

a. It is up to the auctioneer; he or she may do what he or she thinks is best.
b. The answer depends on the type of auction.
c. The auctioneer should honor the seller's wishes and withdraw the item.
d. The auctioneer should ignore the seller's wishes and keep the bidding process going.

4. During bidding, can the current high bidder retract his or her bid?

a. yes
b. no
c. It depends on the type of auction.
d. It is up to the auctioneer.

5. What is an auctioneer's main goal during an auction?

a. to keep things moving quickly
b. to make sure bidders understand the bargains available
c. to make the seller as much money as possible
d. to make sure no one pays more than fair market value for goods

6. Two people come forward claiming to be the high bidder for an item, and both are prepared to pay for the item. It is raining and close to dusk. There is a large crowd, and the two bidders are similar in dress and appearance. For these reasons, the auctioneer and his assistants cannot say for sure which person was actually the high bidder. What should be done in this situation?

a. The item should be put back up for auction at the next highest bid.
b. The auctioneer should ask people in the crowd if they saw who the high bidder was.
c. The auctioneer should flip a coin to decide the winner.
d. The auctioneer should ask the seller to make the decision.

7. At an absolute auction, a seller may bid on his own item.

a. true
b. false

8. A week before an auction, the seller informs the auctioneer that he has arranged for a few of his friends and relatives to act as shills. What should the auctioneer do?

a. The auctioneer should explain that he has his own staff, and that the seller will have to pay the shills out of his own pocket.
b. The auctioneer should ask to meet with them before the auction begins to coordinate things.
c. The auctioneer should explain that this is risky, and should ask for more money upfront to cover the risk.
d. The auctioneer should tell the seller this is unethical, and should threaten to call off the auction unless the seller agrees to cancel his arrangement.

9. One of the items up for sale at an auction is a used car. The auctioneer has never driven the car, but has looked under the hood, started the car, checked out its maintenance history, and had it inspected for mechanical defects. Given these facts, which of these statements would be considered misrepresentation as opposed to acceptable sales hype?

a. "Folks, this car has been well taken care of."
b. "She handles like a dream."
c. "My mechanic gave it two thumbs up."
d. "You'll be the envy of all your neighbors when they see this parked in your driveway."

10. The auctioneer has a contract with the current high bidder.

a. true
b. false

11. A real estate investor who wants to free up some cash may legally hold an auction to sell a 100-unit apartment complex he owns.

a. true
b. false

12. An antique store owner is retiring, and has approached you about auctioning off her remaining inventory. She has already sold much of it; the remaining items will be more difficult to sell. She tells you that she is not that concerned about the prices she gets for the items; she just wants them taken off of her hands. What kind of auction would be best in this situation?

a. minimum bid auction
b. absolute auction
c. reserve auction
d. Yankee auction

13. Two people are bidding vigorously on an antique armoire. One bidder gives up, and you are about to drop the hammer and declare "Sold!" The high bidder suddenly looks confused and announces he has changed his mind and wants to withdraw his bid. What should you do next?

a. Inform him that he cannot withdraw his bid, and that he must pay for the item.
b. Announce that the next highest bidder has won the item based on his last bid.
c. Start the bidding over from the beginning, and let everyone bid.
d. Start the bidding over from the beginning, but refuse to let the man who withdrew his bid to participate.

14. Which of the following is an acceptable reason for an auctioneer to refuse to accept a bid from someone?

a. She thinks the bidder is a shill.
b. She thinks the bidder lacks the funds to pay for the item.
c. She believes the bidder has been drinking.
d. all of the above

15. Bidding has ended for an item. When it is time for the high bidder to pay for the item, he apologizes profusely and says he got caught up in the bidding and went over his budget. He states that he cannot afford to pay for the item. What is the proper procedure in this situation?

a. Start the bidding over and let the matter drop, because oral contracts are not enforceable.
b. Ask him how much he can afford, and then negotiate the best deal you can.
c. Tell him he owes the full amount and you will see him in court.
d. Start the bidding over, and inform him that if the final bid is lower than his bid, he will have to make up the difference.

16. If you start your own auction company, from where do you get an EIN?

a. the Secretary of State
b. the county courthouse
c. the IRS
d. the auctioneer licensing authority in your state

17. Churches, charities, and other non-profit groups often hold auctions to raise money. How often can they do this without having to charge buyers sales taxes?

a. twice a year
b. once a year
c. twice a month
d. once a month

18. If you are a licensed auctioneer and you provide auction services for a non-profit group's tax-exempt auction, you must provide your services free of charge.

a. true
b. false

19. Generally speaking, what is the maximum allowable time period for transferring motor vehicle titles?

a. 5 days
b. 10 days
c. 30 days
d. 60 days

20. Must an auctioneer be a licensed real estate agent in order to sell real estate at an auction?

a. no
b. yes
c. yes for auctioneers first licensed in 2009 or later; no for auctioneers licensed earlier
d. Regulations vary by state.

21. Why don't online auction sites have to use the services of an auctioneer?

a. Government regulations don't apply in cyberspace.
b. They are located offshore to avoid this requirement.
c. These sites do not engage in bid calling.
d. Technically, they are required to have at least one licensed auctioneer on the payroll.

22. Many states require auctioneers to pay into an auctioneer recovery fund. What is the purpose of this fund?

a. It is used to reimburse people who make a claim against an auctioneer.
b. It is used to make loans to auctioneers recovering from a slow economy.
c. It is used to provide health insurance for auctioneers, as long as they are self-employed.
d. It is used to reimburse auctioneers who have had goods stolen at an auction.

23. What is the maximum amount a non-profit group can pay an auctioneer for his or her services at a tax-exempt auction?

a. Auctioneers cannot accept money for services rendered at a tax-exempt auction.
b. $1000
c. 10% of net receipts
d. 20% of gross receipts

24. What is a reciprocal agreement?

a. an agreement in which states honor each other's auctioneer licenses
b. a written contract between a seller and an auctioneer
c. a secret agreement to run up the bidding by using two or more shills
d. an agreement between auctioneers to help each other out if one is too ill to work

25. Do you have to attend auctioneering school to become a licensed auctioneer?

a. yes
b. no
c. It varies by state.
d. Yes, you must attend school if you are younger than 21.

26. An elderly widow wants to sell her farm and move into town to be closer to her children and grandchildren. She is considering selling at auction, but is concerned that she will not get what the farm is worth. What kind of auction would be the best choice to make sure the farm is not sold for too low of a price?

a. reserve auction
b. sealed bid auction
c. minimum bid auction
d. absolute auction

27. You have distributed newspaper ads and flyers for an absolute auction, listing an antique Victrola in mint condition as one of the items to be sold with no reserve. The day of the auction, a large crowd arrives, and many people are there to bid on the Victrola. You decide to save it for last to keep the crowd interested. A few hours into the auction, the owner says he has changed his mind and doesn't want to sell the Victrola. Can he refuse to sell it?

a. No; this is an absolute auction and the item has been advertised, so it must be sold.
b. Yes; he is free to change his mind and refuse to sell it.
c. Yes; he may refuse to sell it, but he must reimburse would-be bidders for their time and travel expenses.
d. The law is unsettled on this matter.

28. At an auction that has been advertised as an absolute auction, what percentage of items can require a minimum bid?

a. 0%
b. 10%
c. 25%
d. 49%

29. A bidder has come to pay for the lot she won. Under which of these circumstances would you *not* collect sales tax from her?

a. She shows you her ordination card and says the purchase is for her church.
b. She shows you her official photo ID from a government job.
c. She shows you her current resale certificate.
d. She shows you her ID verifying that she is an officer of a non-profit group.

30. A gun manufactured in or before what year is considered an antique under federal gun laws?

a. 1958
b. 1928
c. 1898
d. 1848

31. Besides the Secretary of State's office, where should an auctioneer look for liens against tangible personal property?

a. the state sales tax office
b. the state department of commerce office
c. the county tax collector's office
d. the world wide Web

32. What is the law that mainly applies to filing liens against property?

a. Uniform Commercial Code
b. Universal Lending and Finance Code
c. IRS Lien Code
d. Anti-Usury Code

33. What is a quiet title action?

a. a legal maneuver to hide the identity of the true owner of a property
b. a certified letter claiming a lien against a title
c. a normal title transfer from buyer to seller
d. a legal action to remove challenges to a clear title

34. What should an auctioneer do if he or she is presented with a piece of property that has a legitimate lien?

a. The auctioneer should refuse to sell it at auction because of legal liability issues.
b. The auctioneer should contact the lien holder to find out how much is owed on the lien, and should make that the reserve price.
c. The auctioneer should sell it and inform the seller that he or she must make the lien holder whole from the proceeds of the sale.
d. The auctioneer should sell it and inform the buyer that he or she must make a separate deal with the lien holder for a clear title.

35. One item that a seller wants to sell at auction is a table saw in like-new condition. You notice that the serial number is unreadable, and appears to have been deliberately worn down with a grinder. What should you do?

a. Sell it "as is."
b. Refuse to sell it.
c. Let the audience know about the situation before bidding starts.
d. Sell it "as is," but require the buyer to sign a Disclaimer of Provenance certificate.

36. You are preparing for an auction in two weeks when you receive word that the seller has filed for bankruptcy. Does this change anything?

a. Yes; you should demand to get paid before the auction starts.
b. No; you should proceed as usual.
c. Yes; you should cancel the auction.
d. Yes; you should place a lien on the seller's checking account to ensure you get paid.

37. How can you protect yourself against bad checks at auctions?

a. Take a photo of the buyer.
b. Take a photo of the buyer's driver's license.
c. Require the buyer to thumbprint his or her check.
d. all of the above

38. In the majority of states, what is the maximum surcharge an auctioneer can charge bidders who pay for their purchases with a credit card?

a. An auctioneer cannot impose a surcharge in this situation.
b. $10
c. 1.5% of the purchase price
d. 3% of the purchase price

39. It is a federal crime to falsely claim an item has been created by a member of which ethnic group?

a. the Amish
b. Native Americans
c. African Americans
d. all of the above

40. A local gun dealer approaches an auctioneer about the possibility of holding six auctions a year at his premises to help him get rid of excess inventory. If the auctioneer agrees to this proposal, does he or she need a federal firearms license?

a. yes
b. no
c. The answer depends on which state the auctioneer is operating in.
d. The law is unsettled on this matter.

41. An auctioneer *always* acts as an agent for

a. the buyer.
b. the general public.
c. the seller's estate.
d. the seller.

42. Every employee of an auction company who physically handles any of the sale merchandise on the day of an auction must be a licensed auctioneer.

a. true
b. false

43. What is a Dutch auction?

a. an invitation-only auction that is usually held to sell items of very high value, such as works of art
b. an auction in which asking prices start high and go lower, and the first bidder wins
c. an auction in which the auctioneer is allowed to bid by proxy for a third party who cannot attend
d. a commercial auction in which bidders attempt to win business from the seller by offering lower and lower bids

44. How long should an auctioneer hold on to his or her records?

a. six months
b. one year
c. three years
d. seven years

45. You are calling bids for a lot, and you open with an asking price of $300. Bidder A bids $300. Bidder B bids $350. Bidder C bids $400. Bidder A bids $450. Bidder B drops out, but Bidder C bids $475. The action comes down to Bidder A and Bidder C. Bidder C's final bid is $600, and Bidder A winds up being the high bidder with a final bid of $625. Hours later, as you are getting ready to end the auction, Bidder A notifies you that he has been reliably informed that Bidder B was acting as a shill for the seller. You verify that this was indeed the case. The buyer then demands that you write him a check. How much should you make the check out for?

a. $325
b. $200
c. $150
d. $25

46. What is the best method of estimating the actual worth of most items and properties?

a. finding out how much the seller paid for an item or property
b. using the Rule of 72
c. comparing the prices of similar items or properties which have recently sold
d. using your professional expertise to make a determination

47. Which of these is NOT a reason a person who has tried unsuccessfully to sell her own home should consider selling it at auction?

a. The bidding process creates excitement and tends to drive up prices.
b. The auctioneer has a lot of experience in advertising, and can bring in interested buyers.
c. She will save money compared to hiring a real estate agent.
d. She can sell her home fast.

48. The Internet is a suitable place to advertise local auctions.

a. true
b. false

49. What is the difference between "calling bids" and "crying bids"?

a. Licensed auctioneers call bids; ring personnel and other unlicensed employees cry bids.
b. Calling bids is what auctioneers do; crying bids is what bidders do.
c. Calling bids is done indoors; crying bids is done outdoors.
d. There is no difference.

50. Which term refers to an auction that does not take place at the same location where sale items are stored?

a. English auction
b. catalog auction
c. Chinese auction
d. Vickrey auction

Answer Key and Explanations

1. D: Generally speaking, items sold at auction are subject to the same state, county, and/or municipal sales taxes as items sold in retail stores. It is the responsibility of the auctioneer to collect the taxes on goods sold at auction from buyers. Some items are exempt from sales taxes, such as real estate and livestock. Auctioneers are required to forward collected taxes to the proper authorities on a regular basis: usually monthly, quarterly, or annually.

2. D: An escrow service is provided by an impartial third party. The purpose of using an escrow service is to facilitate trust between buyers and sellers and make transactions more reliable. Typically, escrow services are provided by reputable banking or financial firms. The buyer deposits money with the escrow service, and the seller transfers (or allows inspection of) the goods or title to a property to the escrow service. The escrow service receives the payment, and then verifies that the goods (or property) are genuine, are as described, and are the rightful property of the seller. Following these steps, the service will release payment to the seller and transfer the goods or property title to the buyer. This protects both buyers and sellers from fraud.

3. B: Whether or not the item can be withdrawn depends on the type of auction. In an absolute auction, you cannot stop the bidding process, as goods are sold to the highest qualified bidder once bidding has started. The same would be true in a minimum bid auction, because the minimum bid of $100 has been met. However, in a reserve auction, the seller or agent may withdraw the item from bidding, as long as the hammer hasn't fallen.

4. A: In most states, any and all bidders, including the current high bidder, are free to retract/withdraw their bids at any time before the auctioneer declares the sale final and drops the gavel. This is true in both reserve and absolute auctions. People who withdraw bids are not required to give a reason for doing so.

5. C: A seller hires an auctioneer because the seller hopes the auctioneer's services will allow the seller to make more money than if he or she had sold the goods on his or her own. Therefore, making the seller as much money as possible from the auction should always be the auctioneer's primary goal. It is usually best to keep things moving quickly, but that is not the auctioneer's primary goal during an auction. Stressing the availability of bargains may ultimately bring in more money for the seller, but it is not the auctioneer's primary goal in and of itself. While an auctioneer should never be party to any kind of fraud, it is not his or her responsibility to determine whether someone is paying "too much" for an item.

6. A: Situations like this are uncommon, but they do occur from time to time. The proper procedure is to reopen the bidding, starting with the highest undisputed bid, which would be the last bid before the final bid. The following is an example: The final bid for an item was $500, and two people claim to be the high bidder. It is not known which person was actually the high bidder. If the previous bid was $475, then bidding should be reopened with a minimum bid of $475. Of course, an auctioneer and his staff should keep careful track of bidding and bidders so the final bidder can be identified with certainty and situations like the one described above can be avoided.

7. B: An absolute auction is one with no minimum bids and no reserve prices. If an item is put up for bids and a bid of $1 is received, and it is the high bid, then the high bidder becomes the owner of the item. It does not matter how much the seller thought the item was worth or how much he or she wanted for it. This is why sellers (or their agents) are not allowed to bid at their own absolute auctions. Doing so would enable them to essentially set a reserve price by outbidding people who were not bidding as much as the seller had hoped.

8. D: A shill is someone who bids on an item solely to drive up its cost and help the seller get a better price. He or she has no interest in actually purchasing the article. He or she always works on behalf of the seller, and almost always has the seller's approval. The shill may work for pay, or may have personal reasons for taking such actions. Should the shill's bid end up being the final bid, the seller will not expect him or her to pay. Needless to say, this sort of thing is extremely unethical. An auctioneer who knowingly goes along with such a scheme is cheating the honest bidders, and is also risking his or her license.

9. B: Since the auctioneer has never actually driven the car, he or she has no idea how it handles. Assuming the mechanic did say the car was in good working order, saying the mechanic gave it "two thumbs up" is acceptable. Likewise, saying the car has been "well taken care of" is also justified. Whether or not someone driving the car would actually be the envy of their neighbors is debatable, but most people would interpret the statement to simply mean that the car is very nice looking. All of the statements with the exception of b are either based on fact or contain what most people would consider an acceptable (or expected) level of "puffery." However, the statement "handles like a dream" is pretty specific, and the auctioneer has no basis for making such a claim.

10. A: Calling bids is a form of entering into a contract. Once the first bid is made, further bid calling is actually a way of seeking to void the contract with the current high bidder by creating a new contract with someone who is willing to make an even higher bid. So, an accepted bid of $150 from a qualified bidder does constitute an oral contract. However, it is not a very binding contract, as the bidder may withdraw his bid as long as the gavel has not dropped. Likewise, in a reserve auction, the auctioneer may withdraw an item from the auction at the request of the seller, as long as the gavel has not dropped.

11. A: It is perfectly legal to sell an apartment complex by auctioning it off to the highest bidder. Various kinds of real estate, including large multi-unit residential and commercial properties, are sold at auction all the time. Of course, this type of auction would not employ the same process as an auction of household goods, mainly because of the value of the property. Bidding would probably be by invitation only, and all potential bidders would be thoroughly checked out before being accepted as qualified bidders.

12. B: An absolute auction is the best approach in this situation. At an absolute auction, because there are no minimum bids required, bids can start out low. Because there is no reserve, bidders do not have to worry that they will not bid high enough to win. Knowing these things, more people will show up to absolute auctions than to reserve auctions, generally speaking. Yankee auctions are rarely used anymore, and this type of auction would not be appropriate for the situation described.

13. D: The bidding must start over from the beginning. The high bidder withdrew his bid before the gavel dropped, so the contract is void. You cannot simply award the armoire to the next highest bidder, because it appears that the original high bidder was either bidding dishonestly, or was bidding while he was not in full possession of his faculties. In either case, without his bids, the winning bid would probably have been much lower. So, the auctioneer should start over from the beginning, and should inform the original high bidder that no bids will be accepted from him.

14. D: All of the reasons listed are valid ones for refusing to accept a bid from someone, and there are many other possible reasons an auctioneer might take this step. In most places, an auctioneer is free to refuse any bid from anyone without being required to provide a reason.

15. D: Negotiating a deal for an amount lower than the final bid is unethical because it is unfair to the other bidders. You should not let the matter drop, because oral contracts made by bidders most certainly are enforceable. You do not want to be tied up in court. Furthermore, if the buyer cannot pay now, there is a good chance he will not be able to pay in the future, either, and this is not fair to you as the auctioneer or to the seller. The only fair thing to do is to restart the bidding and make the bidder pay the difference between the new final bid and the one he reneged on. This is standard operating procedure in almost all states when something like this happens.

16. C: IRS is the acronym for the Internal Revenue Service, which is the federal agency responsible for collecting taxes. The IRS is the government agency that will assign you an EIN (Employer Identification Number) if you go into business. An EIN functions for a business in much the same way a Social Security number does for an individual.

17. A: These groups are known as 501(c) groups because 501(c) is the section of the IRS code that regulates what they can and cannot do. According to the code, these groups may hold a sales-tax-exempt auction twice a year to auction off goods that were either donated to the group or made by members of the group. Each auction may only last for one day.

18. B: You are not required to provide your auction services free of charge to non-profit groups. Some auctioneers do choose to do so, and it may be possible to claim the service as a charitable donation on your taxes. However, you are free to accept payment for your work.

19. B: In most locales, buyers of motor vehicles must transfer title within 10 days from the date of purchase. This applies to most vehicles a typical auctioneer would be dealing with, including trailers. There are some exceptions, such as government-owned vehicles, dealer-owned vehicles, etc. Therefore, an auctioneer should be sure to check the regulations for his or her state.

20. D: This is an area that is still up in the air when it comes to auctioneering, as more and more real estate is being sold at auction. There is no agreed upon national standard at this point, so it will depend on the state you do business in.

21. C: These sites do not engage in bid calling, so they are not required to use an auctioneer. Since bids are recorded automatically and electronically, there is no need for a live human to monitor the bidding and keep track of who bid how much, etc.

22. A: These funds, which may have slightly different names depending on location, are used by states to reimburse people who have a legitimate claim against an auctioneer. Typically, the auctioneer will pay a fee when he or she is initially licensed, which will go into the fund. If the amount of money in the fund gets too low, then the board may levy another fee on licensed auctioneers to bring the balance back up.

23. D: The Internal Revenue Service says that a person may be paid "a reasonable fee" for providing auction services at a tax-exempt auction. In most areas, anything above 20 percent of the gross receipts would be considered unreasonable.

24. A: Many states have agreements with other states to honor each other's auctioneer licenses. This is a great benefit for auctioneers, especially ones who are located near state lines or specialize in auctioning a particular kind of item. Check with your state to see which states will honor your license.

25. C: This varies by state. In many states, if a person has a certain amount of experience working for an auctioneer and can pass the licensing test, then they do not have to go to school. In other states, all prospective auctioneers must attend auctioneering school. Check with your own state to be sure.

26. A: A reserve auction would be the best way to make sure the widow does not receive less for the farm than it is worth. She can set a reserve price, and if bidding does not reach the reserve, the farm will not be sold. Technically, she could hold a minimum bid auction and make the minimum bid her lowest acceptable price, but holding this type of auction usually results in a lower turnout and fewer bids.

27. B: Yes, he may legally refuse to sell it, although you should strongly discourage him from doing so. The auction is absolute, but no item is legally up for bid until the actual "putting up of the goods" for auction. In other words, if you have begun calling bids for an item at an absolute auction, the seller cannot change his mind. If you haven't, however, he is free to take it out of play. In this scenario, it would be a good idea to try to talk him out of doing this, though. Many in the crowd would likely become angry and leave after you announce the Victrola will not be sold (which you should do right away). This would hurt his profits, and would also have a negative impact on your income and reputation.

28. A: If even one item or lot at an auction has a minimum bid, then it is not an absolute auction, and advertising it as such is an ethical violation for an auctioneer. It is false advertising—a kind of "bait and switch."

29. C: Generally speaking, everyone is required to pay sales tax on goods bought at auction (unless an auction is put on by a non-profit group and the sales are considered tax exempt). Government officials, non-profit workers, and members of the clergy have to pay these taxes just like everyone else. However, if a person owns a business and is buying the goods to resell them, and they have a current resale certificate, they do not have to pay sales tax.

30. C: Firearms manufactured in or before 1898 are considered antiques, and are exempt from most regulations concerning guns. Other guns, such as those with a matchlock or flintlock, may also be exempt, even if they were manufactured after 1898. It is imperative to be very knowledgeable about gun laws if you intend to sell any firearms at auction.

31. C: You should do a search for liens against tangible personal property with the Secretary of State's office, and with the county tax collector's office. Doing so should turn up any and all outstanding liens on a piece of property.

32. A: The Uniform Commercial Code (UCC) is the main law governing the filing of liens. It came about in the early 1950s because there was a need to make the different laws regarding conducting business in various states more uniform. Prior to the adoption of the UCC, laws concerning commercial activity could vary significantly from state to state. This was a concern because so many business transactions involve parties in two or more states.

33. D: A quiet title action is a lawsuit to stop someone from claiming ownership of a title. It is a way of asking the court to declare that one party is the true and lawful owner of a property, and that other claimants have no case.

34. B: Once a lien is verified as legitimate, the proper procedure is to contact the lien holder, explain that the seller wants to sell the property at auction, and ask the lien holder how much money it will take to satisfy the lien. This then becomes the reserve price, below which the item will not be sold. In the case of two or more liens, all lien holders should be contacted. The reserve price would be the total of all the lien amounts.

35. B: You should refuse to sell it. There is a very high likelihood that the table saw was stolen from someone at some point, whether the seller knows that or not. There are no valid reasons for removing a serial number. You could be held liable for selling stolen property if you choose to auction it off.

36. C: You should cancel the auction. A seller filing for bankruptcy prior to an auction changes everything, and you are not qualified to sort out all the details. That is the job of the bankruptcy court. If you go ahead with the auction, you could be found in violation of the "automatic stay" provision of the US Code.

37. D: Ideally, you should take the measures identified in choices a, b, and c when a person pays for an auction lot with a check. If you cannot follow all three of the recommendations, follow as many as you can, because you will need as much evidence as possible should you have to go to court over the matter.

38. A: In most states, it is illegal to impose a surcharge on a customer for using a credit card, even though you must pay a fee to the credit card company every time you take a credit card payment. The merchant agreement you sign with the credit card company also prohibits this practice.

39. B: The following is from the Department of the Interior's Indian Arts and Crafts Page: "The Indian Arts and Crafts Act of 1990 (P.L. 101-644) is a truth-in-advertising law that prohibits misrepresentation in marketing of Indian arts and crafts products within the United States. It is illegal to offer or display for sale, or sell any art or craft product in a manner that falsely suggests it is Indian produced, an Indian product, or the product of a particular Indian or Indian Tribe or Indian arts and crafts organization, resident within the United States. For a first time violation of the Act, an individual can face civil or criminal penalties up to a $250,000 fine or a 5-year prison term, or both."

40. A: While laws that apply to auctioneers who sell an occasional firearm at auction can be confusing, this situation is pretty clear cut. An auctioneer who has an arrangement to auction guns on a regular basis is considered a firearms dealer, and needs to have a federal firearms license.

41. D: An auctioneer acts as an agent for the seller. He or she has responsibilities to bidders, buyers, and the general public, but does not act as their agent. The seller's estate (choice c) is redundant. If an estate has authorized an auction, the estate is the seller.

42. B: A person must be a licensed auctioneer to engage in bid calling, but auction company employees who do not have an auctioneer license may perform tasks such as taking payments, showing the merchandise, assisting the auctioneer, etc.

43. B: A Dutch auction starts with a high initial asking price, which goes lower and lower until a bid is received. The first bidder automatically becomes the winning bidder. The initial asking price in a Dutch auction is usually much higher than the price the seller expects to receive. Dutch auctions are very uncommon.

44. D: Although state record keeping requirements can vary, they usually require an auctioneer to keep records for between three and five years. However, the Internal Revenue Service can audit an individual or a business for activity going back seven years, so an auctioneer should preserve records going back at least this far.

45. A: In a situation where confirmed bad faith bidding drove up the price, the buyer has the right to either void the sale or buy the lot at the "last good faith bid." At first glance, many would say that since C bid $600, $600 was the last good faith bid. However, C did not start bidding until after A had made a bad faith bid of $350. All bids after the first bad faith bid are also considered bad faith bids, and so B is entitled to buy the lot for his last good faith bid of $300. Since he already paid $625, you owe him the difference, which is $325.

46. C: Determining the worth of an item or property is a subjective process. What the seller paid for it originally is irrelevant, unless he or she bought it very recently, which would be unusual. The Rule of 72 is used to estimate how the price or value of an item might change in the future, not to determine its present value. While your experience and expertise can be quite useful, the most accurate way of estimating how much something will sell for is to look at the prices of similar items or goods that recently sold.

47. C: Many people who put a For Sale by Owner (FSBO) sign in front of their house find that selling their own home is a lot harder than they thought it would be. If they turn to an auctioneer, they can sell the home fast, because a good auctioneer knows how to get interested bidders to the auction, and the competition can drive up prices. However, the seller will probably not save money compared to going with a real estate agent, because auctioneers usually charge higher commissions than real estate firms.

48. A: Using the Internet can certainly be an effective way to advertise a local auction. More and more people have stopped looking at newspapers and other kinds of periodicals because they get all their information online. Using your own Web site (and possibly other sites of local or specialized interest) to promote upcoming auctions is becoming more and more important every day.

49. D: There is no difference. The terms "calling bids" and "crying bids" both refer to what an auctioneer does to encourage people to bid on something and keep people apprised of the current high bid. It is also called "chanting." In different areas, one term might be more popular than the other two, but they all have the same meaning.

50. B: A catalog auction is an auction that is not conducted at the same place where the items being sold are stored. This is a great convenience in many cases, and is a necessity in some others. All ads for an upcoming catalog auction should make it clear it is a catalog sale. They should also identify the location where the goods are stored, and should list the days and times interested parties may inspect them before the auction.

How to Overcome Test Anxiety

Just the thought of taking a test is enough to make most people a little nervous. A test is an important event that can have a long-term impact on your future, so it's important to take it seriously and it's natural to feel anxious about performing well. But just because anxiety is normal, that doesn't mean that it's helpful in test taking, or that you should simply accept it as part of your life. Anxiety can have a variety of effects. These effects can be mild, like making you feel slightly nervous, or severe, like blocking your ability to focus or remember even a simple detail.

If you experience test anxiety—whether severe or mild—it's important to know how to beat it. To discover this, first you need to understand what causes test anxiety.

Causes of Test Anxiety

While we often think of anxiety as an uncontrollable emotional state, it can actually be caused by simple, practical things. One of the most common causes of test anxiety is that a person does not feel adequately prepared for their test. This feeling can be the result of many different issues such as poor study habits or lack of organization, but the most common culprit is time management. Starting to study too late, failing to organize your study time to cover all of the material, or being distracted while you study will mean that you're not well prepared for the test. This may lead to cramming the night before, which will cause you to be physically and mentally exhausted for the test. Poor time management also contributes to feelings of stress, fear, and hopelessness as you realize you are not well prepared but don't know what to do about it.

Other times, test anxiety is not related to your preparation for the test but comes from unresolved fear. This may be a past failure on a test, or poor performance on tests in general. It may come from comparing yourself to others who seem to be performing better or from the stress of living up to expectations. Anxiety may be driven by fears of the future—how failure on this test would affect your educational and career goals. These fears are often completely irrational, but they can still negatively impact your test performance.

Elements of Test Anxiety

As mentioned earlier, test anxiety is considered to be an emotional state, but it has physical and mental components as well. Sometimes you may not even realize that you are suffering from test anxiety until you notice the physical symptoms. These can include trembling hands, rapid heartbeat, sweating, nausea, and tense muscles. Extreme anxiety may lead to fainting or vomiting. Obviously, any of these symptoms can have a negative impact on testing. It is important to recognize them as soon as they begin to occur so that you can address the problem before it damages your performance.

The mental components of test anxiety include trouble focusing and inability to remember learned information. During a test, your mind is on high alert, which can help you recall information and stay focused for an extended period of time. However, anxiety interferes with your mind's natural processes, causing you to blank out, even on the questions you know well. The strain of testing during anxiety makes it difficult to stay focused, especially on a test that may take several hours. Extreme anxiety can take a huge mental toll, making it difficult not only to recall test information but even to understand the test questions or pull your thoughts together.

Effects of Test Anxiety

Test anxiety is like a disease—if left untreated, it will get progressively worse. Anxiety leads to poor performance, and this reinforces the feelings of fear and failure, which in turn lead to poor performances on subsequent tests. It can grow from a mild nervousness to a crippling condition. If allowed to progress, test anxiety can have a big impact on your schooling, and consequently on your future.

Test anxiety can spread to other parts of your life. Anxiety on tests can become anxiety in any stressful situation, and blanking on a test can turn into panicking in a job situation. But fortunately, you don't have to let anxiety rule your testing and determine your grades. There are a number of relatively simple steps you can take to move past anxiety and function normally on a test and in the rest of life.

Physical Steps for Beating Test Anxiety

While test anxiety is a serious problem, the good news is that it can be overcome. It doesn't have to control your ability to think and remember information. While it may take time, you can begin taking steps today to beat anxiety.

Just as your first hint that you may be struggling with anxiety comes from the physical symptoms, the first step to treating it is also physical. Rest is crucial for having a clear, strong mind. If you are tired, it is much easier to give in to anxiety. But if you establish good sleep habits, your body and mind will be ready to perform optimally, without the strain of exhaustion. Additionally, sleeping well helps you to retain information better, so you're more likely to recall the answers when you see the test questions.

Getting good sleep means more than going to bed on time. It's important to allow your brain time to relax. Take study breaks from time to time so it doesn't get overworked, and don't study right before bed. Take time to rest your mind before trying to rest your body, or you may find it difficult to fall asleep.

Along with sleep, other aspects of physical health are important in preparing for a test. Good nutrition is vital for good brain function. Sugary foods and drinks may give a burst of energy but this burst is followed by a crash, both physically and emotionally. Instead, fuel your body with protein and vitamin-rich foods.

Also, drink plenty of water. Dehydration can lead to headaches and exhaustion, especially if your brain is already under stress from the rigors of the test. Particularly if your test is a long one, drink water during the breaks. And if possible, take an energy-boosting snack to eat between sections.

Along with sleep and diet, a third important part of physical health is exercise. Maintaining a steady workout schedule is helpful, but even taking 5-minute study breaks to walk can help get your blood pumping faster and clear your head. Exercise also releases endorphins, which contribute to a positive feeling and can help combat test anxiety.

When you nurture your physical health, you are also contributing to your mental health. If your body is healthy, your mind is much more likely to be healthy as well. So take time to rest, nourish your body with healthy food and water, and get moving as much as possible. Taking these physical steps will make you stronger and more able to take the mental steps necessary to overcome test anxiety.

Mental Steps for Beating Test Anxiety

Working on the mental side of test anxiety can be more challenging, but as with the physical side, there are clear steps you can take to overcome it. As mentioned earlier, test anxiety often stems from lack of preparation, so the obvious solution is to prepare for the test. Effective studying may be the most important weapon you have for beating test anxiety, but you can and should employ several other mental tools to combat fear.

First, boost your confidence by reminding yourself of past success—tests or projects that you aced. If you're putting as much effort into preparing for this test as you did for those, there's no reason you should expect to fail here. Work hard to prepare; then trust your preparation.

Second, surround yourself with encouraging people. It can be helpful to find a study group, but be sure that the people you're around will encourage a positive attitude. If you spend time with others who are anxious or cynical, this will only contribute to your own anxiety. Look for others who are motivated to study hard from a desire to succeed, not from a fear of failure.

Third, reward yourself. A test is physically and mentally tiring, even without anxiety, and it can be helpful to have something to look forward to. Plan an activity following the test, regardless of the outcome, such as going to a movie or getting ice cream.

When you are taking the test, if you find yourself beginning to feel anxious, remind yourself that you know the material. Visualize successfully completing the test. Then take a few deep, relaxing breaths and return to it. Work through the questions carefully but with confidence, knowing that you are capable of succeeding.

Developing a healthy mental approach to test taking will also aid in other areas of life. Test anxiety affects more than just the actual test—it can be damaging to your mental health and even contribute to depression. It's important to beat test anxiety before it becomes a problem for more than testing.

Study Strategy

Being prepared for the test is necessary to combat anxiety, but what does being prepared look like? You may study for hours on end and still not feel prepared. What you need is a strategy for test prep. The next few pages outline our recommended steps to help you plan out and conquer the challenge of preparation.

Step 1: Scope Out the Test

Learn everything you can about the format (multiple choice, essay, etc.) and what will be on the test. Gather any study materials, course outlines, or sample exams that may be available. Not only will this help you to prepare, but knowing what to expect can help to alleviate test anxiety.

Step 2: Map Out the Material

Look through the textbook or study guide and make note of how many chapters or sections it has. Then divide these over the time you have. For example, if a book has 15 chapters and you have five days to study, you need to cover three chapters each day. Even better, if you have the time, leave an extra day at the end for overall review after you have gone through the material in depth.

If time is limited, you may need to prioritize the material. Look through it and make note of which sections you think you already have a good grasp on, and which need review. While you are studying, skim quickly through the familiar sections and take more time on the challenging parts. Write out your plan so you don't get lost as you go. Having a written plan also helps you feel more in control of the study, so anxiety is less likely to arise from feeling overwhelmed at the amount to cover.

Step 3: Gather Your Tools

Decide what study method works best for you. Do you prefer to highlight in the book as you study and then go back over the highlighted portions? Or do you type out notes of the important information? Or is it helpful to make flashcards that you can carry with you? Assemble the pens, index cards, highlighters, post-it notes, and any other materials you may need so you won't be distracted by getting up to find things while you study.

If you're having a hard time retaining the information or organizing your notes, experiment with different methods. For example, try color-coding by subject with colored pens, highlighters, or post-it notes. If you learn better by hearing, try recording yourself reading your notes so you can listen while in the car, working out, or simply sitting at your desk. Ask a friend to quiz you from your flashcards, or try teaching someone the material to solidify it in your mind.

Step 4: Create Your Environment

It's important to avoid distractions while you study. This includes both the obvious distractions like visitors and the subtle distractions like an uncomfortable chair (or a too-comfortable couch that makes you want to fall asleep). Set up the best study environment possible: good lighting and a comfortable work area. If background music helps you focus, you may want to turn it on, but otherwise keep the room quiet. If you are using a computer to take notes, be sure you don't have any other windows open, especially applications like social media, games, or anything else that could distract you. Silence your phone and turn off notifications. Be sure to keep water close by so you stay hydrated while you study (but avoid unhealthy drinks and snacks).

Also, take into account the best time of day to study. Are you freshest first thing in the morning? Try to set aside some time then to work through the material. Is your mind clearer in the afternoon or evening? Schedule your study session then. Another method is to study at the same time of day that you will take the test, so that your brain gets used to working on the material at that time and will be ready to focus at test time.

Step 5: Study!

Once you have done all the study preparation, it's time to settle into the actual studying. Sit down, take a few moments to settle your mind so you can focus, and begin to follow your study plan. Don't give in to distractions or let yourself procrastinate. This is your time to prepare so you'll be ready to fearlessly approach the test. Make the most of the time and stay focused.

Of course, you don't want to burn out. If you study too long you may find that you're not retaining the information very well. Take regular study breaks. For example, taking five minutes out of every hour to walk briskly, breathing deeply and swinging your arms, can help your mind stay fresh.

As you get to the end of each chapter or section, it's a good idea to do a quick review. Remind yourself of what you learned and work on any difficult parts. When you feel that you've mastered the material, move on to the next part. At the end of your study session, briefly skim through your notes again.

But while review is helpful, cramming last minute is NOT. If at all possible, work ahead so that you won't need to fit all your study into the last day. Cramming overloads your brain with more information than it can process and retain, and your tired mind may struggle to recall even previously learned information when it is overwhelmed with last-minute study. Also, the urgent nature of cramming and the stress placed on your brain contribute to anxiety. You'll be more likely to go to the test feeling unprepared and having trouble thinking clearly.

So don't cram, and don't stay up late before the test, even just to review your notes at a leisurely pace. Your brain needs rest more than it needs to go over the information again. In fact, plan to finish your studies by noon or early afternoon the day before the test. Give your brain the rest of the day to relax or focus on other things, and get a good night's sleep. Then you will be fresh for the test and better able to recall what you've studied.

Step 6: Take a Practice Test

Many courses offer sample tests, either online or in the study materials. This is an excellent resource to check whether you have mastered the material, as well as to prepare for the test format and environment.

Check the test format ahead of time: the number of questions, the type (multiple choice, free response, etc.), and the time limit. Then create a plan for working through them. For example, if you have 30 minutes to take a 60-question test, your limit is 30 seconds per question. Spend less time on the questions you know well so that you can take more time on the difficult ones.

If you have time to take several practice tests, take the first one open book, with no time limit. Work through the questions at your own pace and make sure you fully understand them. Gradually work up to taking a test under test conditions: sit at a desk with all study materials put away and set a timer. Pace yourself to make sure you finish the test with time to spare and go back to check your answers if you have time.

After each test, check your answers. On the questions you missed, be sure you understand why you missed them. Did you misread the question (tests can use tricky wording)? Did you forget the information? Or was it something you hadn't learned? Go back and study any shaky areas that the practice tests reveal.

Taking these tests not only helps with your grade, but also aids in combating test anxiety. If you're already used to the test conditions, you're less likely to worry about it, and working through tests until you're scoring well gives you a confidence boost. Go through the practice tests until you feel comfortable, and then you can go into the test knowing that you're ready for it.

Test Tips

On test day, you should be confident, knowing that you've prepared well and are ready to answer the questions. But aside from preparation, there are several test day strategies you can employ to maximize your performance.

First, as stated before, get a good night's sleep the night before the test (and for several nights before that, if possible). Go into the test with a fresh, alert mind rather than staying up late to study.

Try not to change too much about your normal routine on the day of the test. It's important to eat a nutritious breakfast, but if you normally don't eat breakfast at all, consider eating just a protein bar. If you're a coffee drinker, go ahead and have your normal coffee. Just make sure you time it so that the caffeine doesn't wear off right in the middle of your test. Avoid sugary beverages, and drink enough water to stay hydrated but not so much that you need a restroom break 10 minutes into the test. If your test isn't first thing in the morning, consider going for a walk or doing a light workout before the test to get your blood flowing.

Allow yourself enough time to get ready, and leave for the test with plenty of time to spare so you won't have the anxiety of scrambling to arrive in time. Another reason to be early is to select a good seat. It's helpful to sit away from doors and windows, which can be distracting. Find a good seat, get out your supplies, and settle your mind before the test begins.

When the test begins, start by going over the instructions carefully, even if you already know what to expect. Make sure you avoid any careless mistakes by following the directions.

Then begin working through the questions, pacing yourself as you've practiced. If you're not sure on an answer, don't spend too much time on it, and don't let it shake your confidence. Either skip it and come back later, or eliminate as many wrong answers as possible and guess among the remaining ones. Don't dwell on these questions as you continue—put them out of your mind and focus on what lies ahead.

Be sure to read all of the answer choices, even if you're sure the first one is the right answer. Sometimes you'll find a better one if you keep reading. But don't second-guess yourself if you do immediately know the answer. Your gut instinct is usually right. Don't let test anxiety rob you of the information you know.

If you have time at the end of the test (and if the test format allows), go back and review your answers. Be cautious about changing any, since your first instinct tends to be correct, but make sure you didn't misread any of the questions or accidentally mark the wrong answer choice. Look over any you skipped and make an educated guess.

At the end, leave the test feeling confident. You've done your best, so don't waste time worrying about your performance or wishing you could change anything. Instead, celebrate the successful completion of this test. And finally, use this test to learn how to deal with anxiety even better next time.

Review Video: Test Anxiety
Visit mometrix.com/academy and enter code: 100340

Important Qualification

Not all anxiety is created equal. If your test anxiety is causing major issues in your life beyond the classroom or testing center, or if you are experiencing troubling physical symptoms related to your anxiety, it may be a sign of a serious physiological or psychological condition. If this sounds like your situation, we strongly encourage you to seek professional help.

Online Resources

Due to our efforts to try to keep this book to a manageable length, we've created a link that will give you access to all of your online resources:

mometrix.com/resources719/auctioneer

It's Your Moment, Let's Celebrate It!

Share your story @mometrixtestpreparation